# Uncover 4 Combo A

Ben Goldstein • Ceri Jones
with Kathryn O'Dell

## Student's Book

# CAMBRIDGE
## UNIVERSITY PRESS

University Printing House, Cambridge CB2 8BS, United Kingdom

One Liberty Plaza, 20th Floor, New York, NY 10006, USA

477 Williamstown Road, Port Melbourne, VIC 3207, Australia

314–321, 3rd Floor, Plot 3, Splendor Forum, Jasola District Centre, New Delhi – 110025, India

79 Anson Road, #06–04/06, Singapore 079906

José Abascal, 56–1°, 28003 Madrid, Spain

Cambridge University Press is part of the University of Cambridge.

It furthers the University's mission by disseminating knowledge in the pursuit of education, learning and research at the highest international levels of excellence.

www.cambridge.org
Information on this title: www.cambridge.org/9781107515147

© Cambridge University Press 2015

This publication is in copyright. Subject to statutory exception and to the provisions of relevant collective licensing agreements, no reproduction of any part may take place without the written permission of Cambridge University Press.

First published 2015

20 19 18 17 16 15 14 13 12 11 10 9 8 7

Printed in Great Britain by CPI Group (UK) Ltd, Croydon CR0 4YY

*A catalog record for this publication is available from the British Library*

ISBN 978-1-107-49353-7 Student's Book 4
ISBN 978-1-107-49357-5 Student's Book with Online Workbook and Online Practice 4
ISBN 978-1-107-51514-7 Combo 4A
ISBN 978-1-107-51515-4 Combo 4B
ISBN 978-1-107-49367-4 Teacher's Book 4
ISBN 978-1-107-49364-3 Workbook with Online Practice 4
ISBN 978-1-107-49392-6 Presentation Plus Disc 4
ISBN 978-1-107-49386-5 Class Audio CDs 4
ISBN 978-1-107-49391-9 DVD 4

Additional resources for this publication at www.cambridge.org/uncover

Cambridge University Press has no responsibility for the persistence or accuracy of URLs for external or third-party internet websites referred to in this publication, and does not guarantee that any content on such websites is, or will remain, accurate or appropriate. Information regarding prices, travel timetables, and other factual information given in this work is correct at the time of first printing but Cambridge University Press does not guarantee the accuracy of such information thereafter.

Art direction, book design, layout services, and photo research: QBS Learning
Audio production: John Marshall Media

# Acknowledgments

Many teachers, coordinators, and educators shared their opinions, their ideas, and their experience to help create *Uncover*. The authors and publisher would like to thank the following people and their schools for their help in shaping the series.

In Mexico:

María Nieves Maldonado Ortiz (Colegio Enrique Rébsamen); Héctor Guzmán Pineda (Liceo Europeo); Alfredo Salas López (Campus Universitario Siglo XXI); Rosalba Millán Martínez (IIPAC [Instituto Torres Quintero A.C.]); Alejandra Rubí Reyes Badillo (ISAS [Instituto San Angel del Sur]); José Enrique Gutiérrez Escalante (Centro Escolar Zama); Gabriela Juárez Hernández (Instituto de Estudios Básicos Amado Nervo); Patricia Morelos Alonso (Instituto Cultural Ingles, S.C.); Martha Patricia Arzate Fernández, (Colegio Valladolid); Teresa González, Eva Marina Sánchez Vega (Colegio Salesiano); María Dolores León Ramírez de Arellano, (Liceo Emperadores Aztecas); Esperanza Medina Cruz (Centro Educativo Francisco Larroyo); Nubia Nelly Martínez García (Salesiano Domingo Savio); Diana Gabriela González Benítez (Colegio Ghandi); Juan Carlos Luna Olmedo (Centro Escolar Zama); Dulce María Pascual Granados (Esc. Juan Palomo Martínez); Roberto González, Fernanda Audirac (Real Life English Center); Rocio Licea (Escuela Fundación Mier y Pesado); Diana Pombo (Great Union Institute); Jacobo Cortés Vázquez (Instituto María P. de Alvarado); Michael John Pryor (Colegio Salesiano Anáhuac Chapalita)

In Brazil:

Renata Condi de Souza (Colégio Rio Branco); Sônia Maria Bernal Leites (Colégio Rio Branco); Élcio Souza (Centro Universitário Anhaguera de São Paulo); Patricia Helena Nero (Private teacher); Célia Elisa Alves de Magalhães (Colégio Cruzeiro-Jacarepaguá); Lilia Beatriz Freitas Gussem (Escola Parque-Gávea); Sandra Maki Kuchiki (Easy Way Idiomas); Lucia Maria Abrão Pereira Lima (Colégio Santa Cruz-São Paulo); Deborah de Castro Ferroz de Lima Pinto (Mundinho Segmento); Clara Vianna Prado (Private teacher); Ligia Maria Fernandes Diniz (Escola Internacional de Alphaville); Penha Aparecida Gaspar Rodrigues (Colégio Salesiano Santa Teresinha); Silvia Castelan (Colégio Santa Catarina de Sena); Marcelo D'Elia (The Kids Club Guarulhos); Malyina Kazue Ono Leal (Colégio Bandeirantes); Nelma de Mattos Santana Alves (Private teacher); Mariana Martins Machado (Britannia Cultural); Lilian Bluvol Vaisman (Curso Oxford); Marcelle Belfort Duarte (Cultura Inglesa-Duque de Caxias); Paulo Dantas (Britannia International English); Anauã Carmo Vilhena (York Language Institute); Michele Amorim Estellita (Lemec – Lassance Modern English Course); Aida Setton (Colégio Uirapuru); Maria Lucia Zaorob (CEL-LEP); Marisa Veiga Lobato (Interlíngua Idiomas); Maria Virgínia Lebrón (Independent consultant ); Maria Luiza Carmo (Colégio Guilherme Dumont Villares/CEL-LEP); Lucia Lima (Independent consultant); Malyina Kazue Ono Leal (Colégio Bandeirantes); Debora Schisler (Seven Idiomas); Helena Nagano (Cultura Inglesa); Alessandra de Campos (Alumni); Maria Lúcia Sciamarelli (Colégio Divina Providência); Catarina Kruppa (Cultura Inglesa); Roberto Costa (Freelance teacher/consultant); Patricia McKay Aronis (CEL-LEP); Claudia Beatriz Cavalieri (By the World Idiomas); Sérgio Lima (Vermont English School); Rita Miranda (IBI – [Instituto Batista de Idiomas]); Maria de Fátima Galery (Britain English School); Marlene Almeida (Teacher Trainer Consultant); Flávia Samarane (Colégio Logosófico); Maria Tereza Vianna (Greenwich Schools); Daniele Brauer (Cultura Inglesa/AMS Idiomas); Allessandra Cierno (Colégio Santa Dorotira); Helga Silva Nelken (Greenwich Schools/Colégio Edna Roriz); Regina Marta Bazzoni (Britain English School); Adriano Reis (Greenwich Schools); Vanessa Silva Freire de Andrade (Private teacher); Nilvane Guimarães (Colégio Santo Agostinho)

In Ecuador:

Santiago Proaño (Independent teacher trainer); Tania Abad (UDLA [Universidad de Las Americas]); Rosario Llerena (Colegio Isaac Newton); Paúl Viteri (Colegio Andino); Diego Maldonado (Central University); Verónica Vera (Colegio Tomás Moro); Mónica Sarauz (Colegio San Gabriel); Carolina Flores (Colegio APCH); Boris Cadena, Vinicio Reyes (Colegio Benalcázar); Deigo Ponce (Colegio Gonzaga); Byron Freire (Colegio Nuestra Señora del Rosario)

The authors and publisher would also like to thank the following contributors, script writers, and collaborators for their inspired work in creating *Uncover*:
Anna Whitcher, Janet Gokay, Kathryn O'Dell, Lynne Robertson and Dana Henricks

| Unit | Vocabulary | Grammar | Listening | Conversation (Useful language) |
|---|---|---|---|---|
| **1 Tell Me About It!** pp. 2–11 | ■ Media ■ Time expressions | ■ Past tense review ■ *used to* and *would* Grammar reference p. 106 | ■ Cell phones were huge! | ■ Expressing interest and disinterest |
| **2 Best Foot Forward** pp. 12–21 | ■ Personal qualities ■ Phrasal verbs related to making progress | ■ Present perfect with present perfect continuous ■ Past perfect with past perfect continuous Grammar reference p. 107 | ■ It's turned into so much more! | ■ Showing concern |
| **3 Planning for the Future** pp. 22–31 | ■ Verbs of the future ■ Achievements | ■ Future review ■ Future continuous and future perfect Grammar reference p. 108 | ■ The waters around you | ■ Expressing cause and effect |
| **4 What's Cooking?** pp. 32–41 | ■ Cooking verbs ■ Adjectives describing foods | ■ First conditional review ■ Zero conditional ■ Second conditional review Grammar reference p. 109 | ■ A taste test | ■ Cooking instructions |
| **5 Fame and Fortune** pp. 42–51 | ■ Verbs expressing opinions ■ Adverbs of degree | ■ Defining and non-defining relative clauses ■ Tag questions Grammar reference p. 110 | ■ I see your point, but... | ■ Making a point |

Unit 1–5 Review Game pp. 52–53

| Writing | Reading | Video | Accuracy and fluency | Speaking outcomes |
|---|---|---|---|---|
| A blog post about an event | Finding the Facts<br>Reading to Write: Crazy About Comics<br>Culture: Cinderella's Closet | Real or Fake?<br>What music and fashion were your parents into?<br>Milan's Fashion Week | Not using *would* or *used to* for one-time events<br>Pronunciation of *used to* | I can . . .<br>talk about my news-watching habits.<br>talk about experiences in the past.<br>talk about habits in the past.<br>talk about a special event. |
| A thank-you email for support | A Natural Born Climber<br>Reading to Write: Thanks for your help!<br>Culture: Leaving Home to Help | Born to Dive<br>How have you helped a friend?<br>Shanghai Heights<br>The House of the Future (CLIL Project p. 116) | Separable and not separable phrasal verbs<br>Syllable stress | I can . . .<br>talk about a person's qualities.<br>talk about recent events.<br>talk about personal experiences.<br>talk about someone who has helped his/her family. |
| An opinion essay | A Career in Space<br>Reading to Write: Leaving School Early<br>Culture: School in the Cloud | What a Waste!<br>Are you saving up for something?<br>Mission: Possible? | Word order for future perfect<br>Elisions with silent *h*<br>Spelling the *-ing* forms | I can . . .<br>talk about people's plans for the future.<br>talk about plans for the near and distant future.<br>make predictions about the future.<br>discuss what schools will be like in the future. |
| An article about a family dish | Food for Thought<br>Reading to Write: A Traditional Dish<br>Culture: Pots and Pans of the Past | The Origin of Argan Oil<br>What would you make if you had to cook for your family?<br>Fruits of the Sea<br>You Are What You Eat (CLIL Project p. 117) | Using simple present with *if*, *when*, and *unless* to talk about the future<br>Word stress with conditionals | I can . . .<br>talk about how to prepare a simple dish.<br>talk about party preferences.<br>discuss imaginary situations in the future.<br>talk about traditional ways of cooking. |
| A comparison/contrast essay | Celebrity Causes<br>Reading to Write: The Book Is Better!<br>Culture: Getting Paid for Your Opinions | A Cool Experiment<br>How do you prepare for a sports event?<br>Trendsetters | Not repeating subjects in relative clauses<br>Intonation with tag questions | I can . . .<br>express opinions about different topics.<br>give reasons why I'd support a cause.<br>ask questions to confirm and find out information.<br>give my opinion about a movie, book, or fashion trend. |

# 1 Tell Me About It!

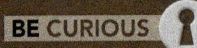

Real or Fake?

What music and fashion were your parents into?

Milan's Fashion Week

1. How much information can you see in this photo? How does it make you feel?

2. How do you get information about local or world events?

3. What important things are happening in your area right now?

**UNIT CONTENTS**

**Vocabulary** Media; Time expressions
**Grammar** Past tense review; Review of *used to* + infinitive and *would*
**Listening** Cell phones were huge!

## Vocabulary: Media

**1. Complete the sentences.**

| article | interview | report |
|---|---|---|
| blogger | ✓ news / the news | reporter |
| headline | paper | review |

**Zoo-mania**
A tiger escaped from the zoo yesterday.

**Escape to Wonder Mountain**
★★★★
*Escape to Wonder Mountain* is an exciting action film that takes place in Canada.

1. I watch ___the news___ on TV every night. My brother gets his ___news___ online.
2. Did you see the big _____ in today's _____? The _____ is about a tiger escaping from the zoo.
3. The _____ did an _____ with a local teen about a neighborhood fire.
4. I'm going to read the _____ before I go see that movie.
5. The _____ wrote about common trends in teen fashion on her website. She included a _____ about the most popular places to shop.

 **2. Listen, check, and repeat.**

**3.** Work with a partner. Put the words from Exercise 1 in the correct categories. Some words can go in more than one category.

| Things you read | Things you watch | Things you listen to | People |
|---|---|---|---|
| article | | | |

## Speaking: My news

**4. YOUR TURN** Work with a partner. When was the last time you did each of these things? Explain what each one was about.

- ☐ watched the news on TV
- ☐ watched the news online
- ☐ read an article in the paper
- ☐ read a review of a product, movie, or music album
- ☐ read or watched an interview

*I watched the news on TV last night. I saw a report about . . .*

▶ Workbook, p. 2

**Reading** Finding the Facts; Crazy About Comics; Cinderella's Closet
**Conversation** Expressing interest and disinterest
**Writing** A blog post about an event

# It isn't always NEWS.

## FINDING THE FACTS

You worked hard on your report for school. You read articles online. You even watched online videos. You thought you did well, but you got the report back from your teacher, and she said that you had to do it again. What did you do wrong? Well, when you were doing your research, you believed everything that was written on the Internet!

A lot of information on the Internet isn't true. Anyone can post information online. A lot of news *looks* real, but contains false information. Sometimes, an article is entirely false. Fake photographs have even been posted with some news stories. Because of this common problem, many websites have been developed to give people true information.

Snopes.com gives people information about urban legends, myths, and other false stories. Many people have used the website to find out whether a story is true or false. For example, there have been a lot of stories online that said that Bill Gates was giving people free laptops. However, Snopes.com reported this wasn't true.

Factcheck.org gives true information about what leaders in the United States say and do. It tells readers when stories aren't true. People who work at Factcheck.org believe that reporters should be honest all of the time and that the news should always be true.

Do you want true information about a person or event in history? WhoWhatWhen gives information about famous people and events from 1000 AD to today. You can even create a timeline of events based on a famous person's life. Do you want to know if the television was invented during Gandhi's lifetime? WhoWhatWhen can tell you!

Be careful when you write reports and use the Internet for research. Check your facts on websites like these and other sites that you know have true information!

### DID YOU KNOW...?
Some websites create false news stories as a joke. These are called *satire websites*.

## Reading: An article about checking facts

1. Look at the title and the pictures. Why do you think the boy might have to write his report again?

2.  Read and listen to the article. What should students do before they write a report?

3. Read the article again. Answer the questions.

   1. Why is there a lot of false information on the Internet?

      _____

   2. Which fact-checking website would you use to find out if something the current US president said were true?

      _____

   3. Which website could you use to find out if it were possible for Elvis Presley to use a computer?

      _____

   4. Which website tells whether an urban legend is true or false?

      _____

4. **YOUR TURN** Work with a partner. What false stories have you read or heard about?

   *I read that you can charge your smartphone with an onion, but it isn't true.*

# Grammar: Past tense review

**5. Complete the chart.**

## Simple past
*Use simple past statements to talk about past events and activities.*

| Regular | Irregular |
|---|---|
| What **did** you **believe**?<br>I _____ everything on the Internet.<br>We **didn't believe** the story. | What _____ she **write**?<br>She **wrote** a report for school.<br>She **didn't write** a blog post. |

## Past continuous
*Use the past continuous to talk about activities that were in progress in the past. To form the past continuous use was/were + present participle (-ing form).*

What _____ you _____ wrong?
I **was using** incorrect information. I **wasn't checking** my facts.

## Present perfect
*Use the present perfect to talk about experiences that happened at an indefinite time in the past. To form the present perfect, use has/have + the past participle.*

Who **has used** Snopes.com?
Many people _____ the website! I **haven't used** it before.

 Check your answers: Grammar reference, p. 106

**6. Complete the conversations with the correct form of the verbs in the questions. ✓ = yes, ✗ = no.**

1. **A:** What were you watching last night?
   **B:** I _was watching_ (✓) the news. I _____ (✗) a movie.
2. **A:** Who has seen my keys?
   **B:** Peter _____ (✓) them. He _____ (✗) them today, though.
3. **A:** Where did Jackie go?
   **B:** She _____ (✓) to the store. She _____ (✗) to the market.
4. **A:** What were Tom and Jill posting online last night?
   **B:** They _____ (✓) a video. They _____ (✗) photos.

**7. Write sentences. Use the form in parentheses.**

1. the TV show / recorded / in April (past passive)
   _The TV show was recorded in April._
2. the papers / not deliver (present perfect passive)
   _____
3. the report / file / in the main office (past passive)
   _____
4. the letters / open (present perfect passive)
   _____
5. the name of the reporter / not give (past passive)
   _____

### Past passive and present perfect passive
*Use the passive when it is not important who does the action, or when you don't know who does it.*

**Past passive**
*To form the past passive, use* was/were + *past participle.*
The television **was invented** during Gandhi's lifetime. It **wasn't invented** during Abraham Lincoln's lifetime.

**Present perfect passive**
*To form the present perfect passive, use* has/have + been + *past participle.*
Fake photographs **have been posted** online. They **haven't been printed** in our newspaper.

# Speaking: A newsworthy event

**8. YOUR TURN** Work with a partner. Talk about a time you did or saw something special on vacation.

> I went to a music festival last summer. It was in . . .

 **BE CURIOUS** Find out about fake news and photos. How has technology changed the way we share information? (Workbook, p. 73)

1.1 REAL OR FAKE?

 Workbook, p. 3

# What Life WAS LIKE

## Listening: Cell phones were huge!

1. Have you ever talked to your parents about what technology was like when they were young? How was it different from today?

2. Listen to Brandon talk to his mom about technology in the past. Check (✓) the things his mom DIDN'T have in high school.

   ☐ a smartphone   ☐ a phone in her room   ☐ a computer   ☐ a color TV

3. Listen again. Are the sentences true or false? Write *T* (true), *F* (false), or *NI* (no information).

   1. Brandon and his mom often watch old movies. ____
   2. Brandon's mom's best friend had a cell phone. ____
   3. Brandon's mom has a smartphone now. ____
   4. Brandon's mom had a computer in college. ____
   5. Brandon's mom did research at the library. ____
   6. Brandon's mom watched the news by herself. ____

## Vocabulary: Time expressions

4. Underline the event that happened first. If the events happened at the same time, underline them both.

   1. I bought a new phone **after** <u>I lost my old one</u>.
   2. **As** I was watching a movie, my brother was playing a video game.
   3. I called Rick **as soon as** I found out the game was canceled.
   4. **Before** my dad left for work, he read the paper.
   5. **By the time** I got to the party, my friends were gone.
   6. **Every time** I had difficult homework, I asked my sister for help.
   7. I've watched video clips **since** my friend started posting them.
   8. I studied at the library **until** it was dark.
   9. **When** I got to the café, I sent Julia a text.
   10. **Whenever** I get together with my best friend, I feel happy.
   11. I read some reviews **while** I was online.

5. **YOUR TURN** Complete the sentences with a time expression from Exercise 4 and your own information.

   1. I've had a smartphone  *since I was 12* .
   2. _____ something exciting happens, I call _____.
   3. _____ I turn 20, I _____.
   4. _____ I see my best friend, we _____.
   5. I do research online _____.

# Grammar: Review of *used to* + infinitive and *would*

**6. Complete the chart.**

| Use *used to* or *would* for things that happened repeatedly in the past but don't happen now. | |
|---|---|
| Where **did** she **use to do** research?<br>She _____ **to do** it at the library.<br>She **didn't use to have** a computer. | **Did** you _____ **to go** to the library?<br>Yes, I **did**.<br>No, I **didn't**. |
| When **would** you **watch** the news?<br>I _____ it at 6:00.<br>I **wouldn't watch** it online. | _____ they **watch** the news every night?<br>Yes, they **would**.<br>No, they **wouldn't**. |
| Use *used to*, not *would*, for situations that happened in the past. | |
| I **used to live** in Los Angeles. (NOT: ~~I would live~~ in Los Angeles.) | |

> Check your answers: Grammar reference, p. 106

**7. Complete the sentences with *would* when possible. When not possible, use *used to*.**

My cousin ¹ _used to live_ (live) on a farm when he was a boy. As soon as he got up, he ² _____ (feed) the animals. He ³ _____ (not have) a computer or a smartphone when he was young. Every time he wanted to use a computer, he ⁴ _____ (go) to the library. I ⁵ _____ (not talk) to my cousin very much, but I ⁶ _____ (visit) him in the country sometimes. We ⁷ _____ (not play) inside – we were always outside. My sister and I ⁸ _____ (help) him with the animals. He ⁹ _____ (come) to our house in the city, too. He ¹⁰ _____ (love) playing my video games. When we got older, we ¹¹ _____ (not see) each other very much. I moved to the country, and my cousin moved to the city! Now, we both live in the city and see each other whenever we can. Where ¹² _____ (you / live) when you were young?

**8. Rewrite the sentences. Change *used to* to *would*. If it's not possible, write X.**

1. I used to swim every summer. _I would swim every summer._
2. Ellen used to be on a soccer team. _____
3. Jack and Terry used to play video games for hours. _____
4. I didn't use to have a phone in my room. _____
5. We didn't use to sleep late on the weekends. _____
6. Did you use to walk to school every day? _____
7. Where did Sara use to live? _____
8. When did they use to go on vacation? _____

> **Get it RIGHT!**
> Do not use **would** or **used to** for an event that happened once.
> I **watched** the news at 6:00 last night.
> (NOT: ~~I would watch the news at 6:00 last night.~~ ~~I used to watch the news at 6:00 last night.~~)

# Speaking: My life in the past

**9.**  **Work with a partner. Talk about your life 10 years ago. How does it compare to now? Use the ideas in the box and your own ideas.**

| how you got to school | what technology you used/had |
| activities you did at school | what you did on the weekends |

> I used to walk to school every day because I lived close to the school. But then we moved, so now I take the bus.

> I used public transportation when I was a kid. I would take the subway, and I take it now, too.

> **Say it RIGHT!**
> In sentences with **used to**, the **d** in *used* is often not pronounced and the **s** makes the /s/ sound.
> With **used** in the simple past, the **d** is pronounced and the **s** makes the /z/ sound. Listen to the differences in the sentences.
> She **used** to walk to school every day.
> He **used** public transportation.
> Pay attention to the way you say **used to** in Exercise 9.

 **REAL TALK** 1.2 WHAT MUSIC AND FASHION WERE YOUR PARENTS INTO?

# Interests
# NOW and THEN

## Conversation: Interests change.

 1. **REAL TALK** Watch or listen to the teenagers talk about their parents' music and fashion in the past. Number the topics in the order you hear them.

_____ liked Michael Jackson          _____ liked the Beatles
_____ liked punk music               _____ liked pop music
_____ used to wear dresses with bows _____ probably liked disco
_____ didn't like anything popular   _____ used to have pink hair

2. **YOUR TURN** What music and fashion were *your* parents into when they were growing up? Tell your partner.

 3. Listen to Liz and Ivan talk about music. Complete the conversation.

**USEFUL LANGUAGE: Expressing interest and disinterest**

| crazy about | ✓ really into | all about |
| not crazy about | not that into | can't stand |

**Liz:** I like your hair, Ivan.
**Ivan:** Thanks. I'm ¹ *really into* the punk look right now. The music, too.
**Liz:** What bands do you listen to?
**Ivan:** Well, I'm ² _____ the punk bands today. My mom used to listen to punk music, so I listen to all the bands she liked in the 1970s.
**Liz:** That's cool.
**Ivan:** What kind of music do you like?
**Liz:** Well, last year I was ³ _____ pop music, but this year I'm ⁴ _____ it. I listen to a lot of rap these days.
**Ivan:** I see. It's funny how interests change. Last year, I didn't know what punk music was, and now I'm ⁵ _____ it!
**Liz:** So what did you listen to last year?
**Ivan:** Rap music! Sorry, Liz, but now I ⁶ _____ it!
**Liz:** That's OK.

4. Practice the conversation with a partner.

5. **YOUR TURN** Work with a partner. Talk about your interests in the past and today. Use the situations in the chart or your own ideas.

| What | When |
|---|---|
| music | last year and this year |
| fashion | five years ago and this year |
| sports/games | eight years ago and now |

*I'm really into rock music.*

*What bands do you listen to?*

*Last year, I really liked this local band, Volcanic Fire. But this year, I'm all about rock bands from the '80s like Joan Jett and the Blackhearts.*

# CRAZY ABOUT COMICS

by Brian Campbell

I went to Comic-Con International in San Diego by myself last Saturday. It's an event for people who are crazy about comic books.

As soon as I got there, I went to a discussion group. Five comic book writers were talking about their comics. As I was leaving the room, I met one of the writers. It was an amazing experience because I myself hope to be a comic book writer someday! After that, I met a friend, and we bought comic books for ourselves. Some people who go to Comic-Con dress up as their favorite characters. I used to dress up as Rocket Raccoon, but this year, I went as Spider-Man. Comic-Con International is an amazing event. The best thing about it is meeting new people with similar interests.

Next year, Comic-Con International is in July. There are also Comic-Con events all over the world.

## Reading to write: A blog post about an event

6. Look at the photo. What event do you think Brian went to? Read his blog post to check.

> ### Focus on CONTENT
> When you write about an event, present the information in this order:
> 1. Give general information about the event.
> 2. Give details about what you did or saw.
> 3. Give your opinion about the event.
> 4. Give information about the event in the future or similar events.

7. Read Brian's blog post again. What is the event? What did Brian do there? What does he think about the event?

> ### Focus on LANGUAGE
> You can use *reflexive* and *emphatic pronouns* in blogs. Use *emphatic pronouns* to emphasize a noun.
>
> | Reflexive | Emphatic |
> |---|---|
> | myself | I myself |
> | yourself / yourselves | you yourself / you yourselves |
> | herself / himself | she herself / he himself |
> | ourselves | we ourselves |
> | themselves | they themselves |
>
> I made dinner **myself**. My **mother herself** said it was delicious!

8. Find the reflexive and emphatic pronouns in Brian's blog.

9. Complete the sentences with pronouns from the Focus on Language box.

   1. The comic book writer _____ said that he was going to introduce a new character.
   2. I bought _____ three new video games.
   3. Lauren and Rafa learned about the problem _____ by reading articles online.
   4. We watched _____ in a video last night.
   5. You _____ said that the concert was boring.

## Writing: Your blog post about an event

### PLAN
You are going to write a blog post about an event. Think of an event you went to and write notes about it.

| | |
|---|---|
| Name of the event | |
| Brief description of the event | |
| What you did or saw | |
| Your opinion of it | |
| Information about future or similar events | |

### WRITE
Write your blog post. Use your notes to help you. Write at least 125 words.

### CHECK
Check your writing. Can you answer "yes" to these questions?

- Is information from the Focus on Content box in your blog post?
- Do you use reflexive and emphatic pronouns correctly?

# Cinderella's Closet

Prom is a big dance that students in the United States go to in their last two years of high school. Girls usually wear beautiful dresses and boys often wear tuxedos. Prom can be very expensive, and some students can't afford the dresses and tuxedos. Two high school students, Stephanie Tomasetta and Katie Adams, wanted to change that.

Stephanie and Katie's organization, Cinderella's Closet, provides dresses and tuxedos for high school students in New Jersey who don't have enough money for prom clothes. They now have over 1,200 prom dresses. Each year, boys and girls come to "shop" for dresses and tuxedos. They wear them to prom and then return them. They also get shoes and jewelry. In 2014, over 500 students borrowed clothes for prom. Stephanie and Katie knew how to make the event special. Over 150 volunteers helped with the event. Most of the volunteers were high school students. Some of them were "personal shoppers." They helped other teens pick out clothing. Other volunteers gave girls advice on makeup.

Cinderella's Closet needs a lot of money for the dresses and tuxedos. For the past several years, Stephanie and Katie have become experts at raising money. One way they raise money is with a fashion show every year. People who attend the fashion show donate money. In 2014, they raised $40,000. It was a special event because teenagers designed and made the outfits for the show. About 40 high school boys and girls modeled the fashions for a big crowd. The audience voted on the best design. People who work in fashion also voted and gave several awards to the student designers.

Stephanie and Katie say that Cinderella's Closet isn't just about beautiful clothing. It's about making teenagers feel good about themselves, too.

## Culture: An organization for prom fashions

1. Look at the photos and the title of the article. What do you think Cinderella's Closet is?

2. Read and listen to the article. Why did Stephanie and Katie start Cinderella's Closet?

3. Read the article again. Check (✓) the things that teenagers do for Cinderella's Closet.

   ☐ They sell dresses and tuxedos to students.
   ☐ They lend dresses and tuxedos to students.
   ☐ They volunteer and help other teens look for dresses.
   ☐ They donate money to the organization.
   ☐ They design clothes for the fashion show.
   ☐ They model at the fashion show.
   ☐ They work in fashion and voted at the fashion show.

4. **YOUR TURN** Work with a partner. What special dances or other events do you have at your school? What do teens wear or do for the events?

### DID YOU KNOW...?
For some proms, students decorate their high school gyms for the dance. Other proms are at fancy hotels.

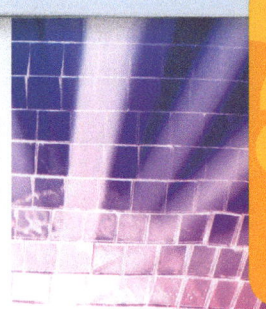

BE CURIOUS — Find out about the Milan Fashion Show. Does the blogger want to be a model? Why or why not? (Workbook, p. 74)

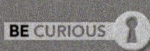

1.3 MILAN'S FASHION WEEK

# UNIT 1 REVIEW

## Vocabulary

1. **Circle the correct answers.**
   1. As soon as I got home, I watched **the news** / **the article** on TV.
   2. After I wrote **a report** / **a reporter** for class, I emailed it to my teacher.
   3. I want to be **a headline** / **a reporter** for the school **paper** / **review** next year.
   4. My brother only reads the **headlines** / **paper**, but I like to read the entire **article** / **blogger**.
   5. Before I buy something online, I always read the **interview** / **reviews**.
   6. My aunt is **a report** / **a blogger**, and she does **interviews** / **news** with community members and then writes posts about them on her website.

## Grammar

2. **Rewrite the sentences. Use the tense in parentheses.**
   1. I worked a lot yesterday. (past continuous)
      *I was working a lot yesterday.*
   2. Tara didn't pass her test. (present perfect)
      _____
   3. They wrote the story in two days. (past passive)
      _____
   4. Ricky works for a TV station. (simple past)
      _____
   5. Are you reading an interesting article? (past continuous)
      _____
   6. They have written the report in three languages. (present perfect passive)
      _____

3. **Complete the sentences with *would* when possible. When not possible, use *used to*.**
   1. When I was younger, I _would watch_ (watch) videos online. I _____ (look) at them all day long. I _____ (be) crazy about animal videos.
   2. My cousin _____ (live) in San Diego, but now he's in Denver. In San Diego, he _____ (go) to Comic-Con every year. He _____ (have) a comic book collection, but he sold it a few years ago.
   3. _____ (you / be) a reporter for your school paper? _____ (you / write) articles about important issues?

## Useful language

4. **Circle the correct responses to complete the conversations.**
   1. **A:** Do you like punk music?
      **B:** ____. It's too loud, and I don't understand the words.
      a. I'm crazy about it.
      b. I'm not crazy about it.
   2. **A:** What do you think of big sunglasses?
      **B:** ____. I have three pairs!
      a. I'm really into them.
      b. I'm not really into them.
   3. **A:** What sports do you like to watch?
      **B:** ____. I like all the games, and I especially like the World Cup.
      a. I'm all about soccer.
      b. I can't stand soccer.

---

**PROGRESS CHECK: Now I can . . .**

- ☐ talk about my news-watching habits.
- ☐ talk about experiences in the past.
- ☐ talk about habits in the past.
- ☐ express interest and disinterest.
- ☐ write about an event.
- ☐ talk about a special event.

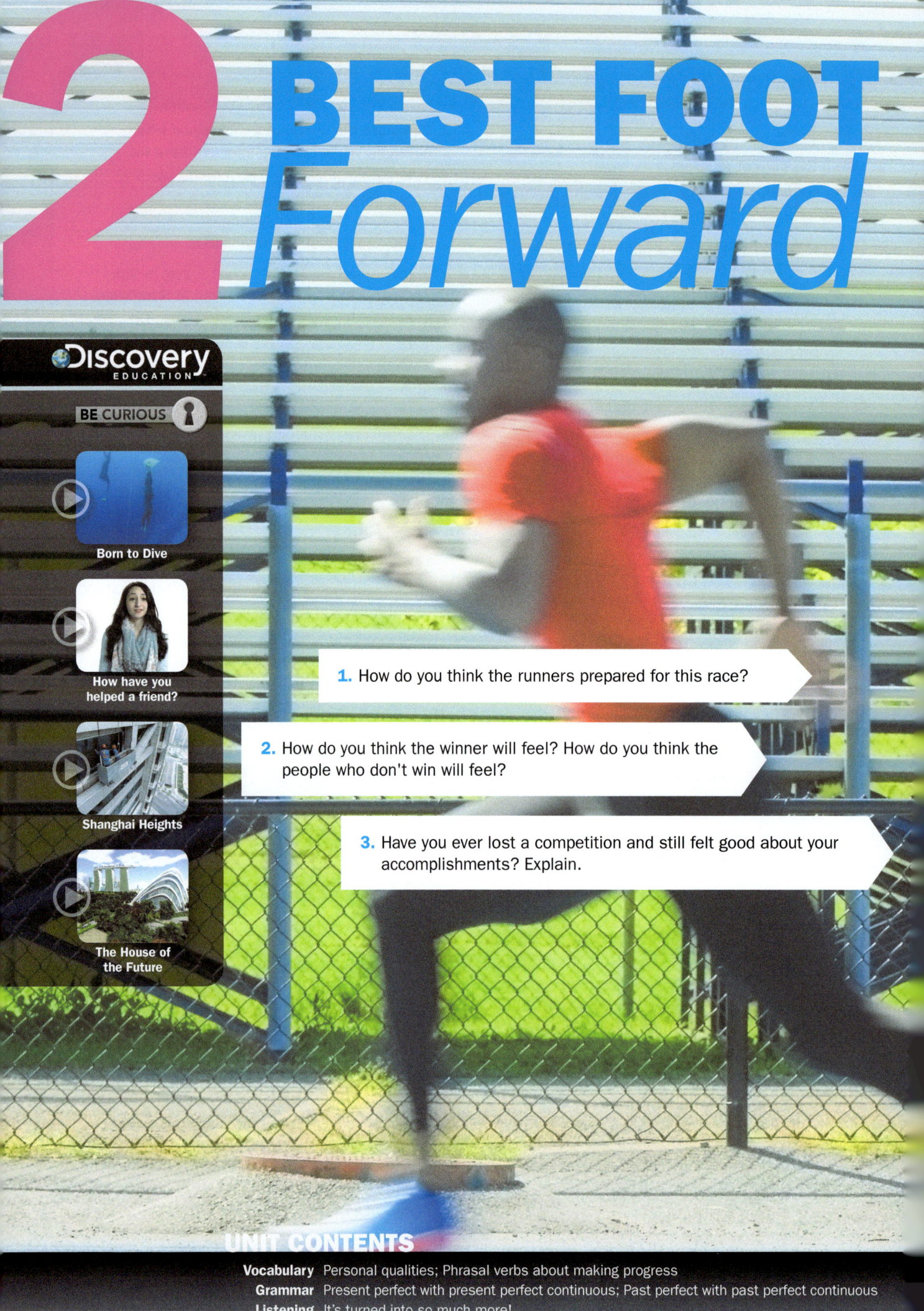

# 2 BEST FOOT Forward

**Discovery EDUCATION — BE CURIOUS**
- Born to Dive
- How have you helped a friend?
- Shanghai Heights
- The House of the Future

1. How do you think the runners prepared for this race?

2. How do you think the winner will feel? How do you think the people who don't win will feel?

3. Have you ever lost a competition and still felt good about your accomplishments? Explain.

**UNIT CONTENTS**
**Vocabulary** Personal qualities; Phrasal verbs about making progress
**Grammar** Present perfect with present perfect continuous; Past perfect with past perfect continuous
**Listening** It's turned into so much more!

## Vocabulary: Personal qualities

**1. Match the sentences with the correct pictures.**

a
b
c
d
e

1. __c__ She's very **talented**. Her pictures are really beautiful. And she's **determined**, too. She tries again and again until she gets it just right.
2. _____ He's really fun, and he's very **sociable**. He talks with everyone. He's really good with the **shy** kids, too – the ones who don't want to talk.
3. _____ He's **strict** and he makes his students work hard, but they love him and are very **motivated**.
4. _____ She's **passionate** about dancing. She loves it! And she's very **hardworking**, too. She spends all her free time at the dance studio.
5. _____ She's very **easy-going**. She never gets angry or **impatient** that I haven't practiced. And I'm not very good, so she has to be really patient!

 **2. Listen, check, and repeat.**

 **3. Listen to people describing themselves. Match them to the personal qualities in Exercise 1.**

1. _motivated_  5. _____  9. _____
2. _____  6. _____  10. _____
3. _____  7. _____
4. _____  8. _____

 **Say it RIGHT!**

In words with more than one syllable, one of the syllables is stressed more than the others. Listen to the stress in these words.

mo-ti-**va**-ted    de-**ter**-mined

Listen to the rest of the words from Exercise 1 with more than one syllable. Which syllables are stressed?

## Speaking: My helper

**4. YOUR TURN** Work with a partner. Think of a person who helps you in some way. Choose three adjectives from Exercise 1 that describe him or her. Tell your partner about the person.

_My older brother helps me with my homework. He's very patient and . . ._

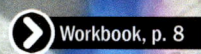 Workbook, p. 8

**Reading** A Natural Born Climber; Thanks for your help!; Leaving Home to Help
**Conversation** Showing concern
**Writing** A thank-you email for support

Unit 2 | 13

# It's **HARD** work!

## A NATURAL BORN CLIMBER

Brooke Raboutou has just turned 12, and she is one of the best rock climbers in the world, with seven world records. One of her coaches explains why she's so good. "She has incredibly strong fingers," he says. He adds that she also has the flexibility of a child. This really helps in climbing. It means she can do things older climbers have never dreamed of doing. Practice also helps. Brooke has been climbing regularly since she was four years old.

Brooke comes from a climbing family. Both of her parents are climbing champions. Her father has stopped climbing, but her mother, Robyn, who won the World Cup title four years in a row, is still climbing. She has been running a club for young climbers in Colorado since 2005. She coaches Brooke and her teammates. Brooke says her mom is a great coach. "She encourages me a lot. She gives me really good advice," Brooke says. "She's just a big part of my climbing life." Robyn can be strict, but she is also passionate. She has been passing this passion on to her daughter and students for years.

Brooke is very determined and has always been very motivated. This helps her when she's facing the challenges of this difficult sport. She's also hardworking. She hasn't gotten to the top of her sport by sitting around. "To be a really good climber, you can't just have it. You have to train really hard, so I take it pretty seriously," Brooke says. And that's what Brooke has been doing every day, at the club and at home. She even has a climbing wall in her basement.

But climbing isn't only hard work. It's fun, too. "When I'm on a high rock, I feel in control and just happy," Brooke says. "And when I look down, I'm not scared because I'm not scared of heights. But it's just so cool to think how small I am compared to the rock and how high up I am."

## Reading: An article about a young rock climber

1. Look at the title and the picture. What do you think are three adjectives that describe Brooke?

2.  Read and listen to the article. How does Brooke feel about rock climbing?

3. Read the article again. Answer the questions.
   1. What makes Brooke a good climber?
      _____
   2. What is Brooke's parents' connection to rock climbing?
      _____
   3. What does Brooke's mom do now?
      _____
   4. Why does Brooke think her mom is good at her job?
      _____
   5. How does Brooke feel when she's up high on a rock?
      _____

4. **YOUR TURN** Work with a partner. Have you tried rock climbing? What was it like? If not, would you like to try it? Explain.

### DID YOU KNOW...?
Rock climbing has been a sport for more than 150 years.

# Grammar: Present perfect with present perfect continuous

### 5. Complete the chart.

| Present perfect continuous |  |
|---|---|
| *Use the present perfect continuous for experiences that happened at an indefinite time in the past and continue to the present.* | |
| Where **have** you **been climbing**? <br> I _____ at the club. <br> I **haven't been climbing** in the mountains. | **Have** you **been training** a lot? <br> Yes, I **have**. <br> No, I _____. |
| What **has** she **been doing**? <br> She **has been running** a club. <br> She _____ **working** in an office. | _____ she _____ **climbing** for a long time? <br> Yes, she **has**. <br> No, she **hasn't**. |
| **Present perfect vs. present perfect continuous** | |
| *Remember to use the present perfect for experiences that happened at an indefinite time in the past and are now complete. Use the present perfect to emphasize the result.* | |
| He used to be a professional rock climber, but he _____ **stopped** climbing. | |
| *Use the present perfect continuous to emphasize the action.* | |
| She _____ **climbing** since she was four. | |

> Check your answers: Grammar reference, p. 107

### 6. Write sentences with the present perfect continuous.

1. Cara / take / swimming lessons for six years  *Cara has been taking swimming lessons for six years.*
2. they / work / here since 2013  _____
3. you / not live / in Vancouver for very long  _____
4. Ricardo / text / Maria all day  _____

### 7. Use the present perfect continuous when possible. When not possible, use the present perfect.

1. Olivia *hasn't finished* (not finish) high school yet.
2. She _____ (study) dance for three years.
3. She _____ (be) motivated all of her life.
4. Her parents _____ (help) her follow her dream of becoming a famous dancer.
5. They _____ just _____ (save) enough money for her to go to a dance school in New York City.
6. _____ you ever _____ (know) someone who followed their dreams?

> *Use the present perfect, not the present perfect continuous, with ever, never, just, already, and yet.*
> 
> She **has already won** four competitions.
> (NOT: ~~She's already been winning~~ . . .)
> 
> *Use the present perfect, not the present continuous, with know, have, and be.*
> 
> I **have known** Brooke for many years.
> (NOT: ~~I have been knowing~~ Brooke . . .)

# Speaking: What have you been doing?

### 8. YOUR TURN Work with a partner. Ask and answer questions about something you've been learning to do recently.

- How long have you been learning it?
- Why did you start?
- Who has been teaching you?
- What has been the most difficult thing to learn?

*I've been taking piano lessons every weekend.*

*Have you been taking them for very long?*

> Workbook, p. 9

**BE CURIOUS** Find out about a free diver. What is free diving? (Workbook, p. 74)

Discovery EDUCATION

2.1 BORN TO DIVE

# Helping HANDS

## Listening: It's turned into so much more!

1. Have you ever taught someone how to do something? Was it difficult or easy?

 2. Listen to an interview about a program a teenager started. What's the name of the program? What's its purpose?

3. Listen again. Answer the questions.
   1. Who are the teachers? Who are the students?
   2. How many people were in the program last year? How many are in it this year?
   3. What do the students learn to do? What do the teachers learn from the students?
   4. What was Helen's job in the past? What did she do at her job?
   5. Why is Jake surprised?

## Vocabulary: Phrasal verbs about making progress

 4. Read the sentences. Match the words with the definitions. Then listen and check.

1. __g__ This project can **bring together** students and older people.
2. _____ I hope my music hobby will **turn into** a career!
3. _____ My grandmother wants to **sign up** for computer lessons.
4. _____ They want to **keep up** with their grandkids.
5. _____ We help them **set up** social networking pages.
6. _____ We don't want them to **give up**.
7. _____ We **get along** with each other.
8. _____ They **pass on** their knowledge to young people.
9. _____ They **count on** us to help them.

a. to stop doing something
b. to give something to someone
c. to arrange to do an organized activity
d. to have a good relationship (with someone)
e. to get things ready for something
f. to depend on someone or something
g. to cause people to join each other
h. to become something different
i. to stay equal (with someone)

> **Get it RIGHT!**
> Some phrasal verbs are separable. An object can go after the preposition or between the verb and the preposition.
> We helped **set up** the site.
> We helped **set** the site **up**.
> Some phrasal verbs are not separable.
> They **count on** volunteers to help.
> (NOT: They ~~count~~ volunteers ~~on~~ to help.)

5. **YOUR TURN** Work with a partner. Ask and answer questions using phrasal verbs from Exercise 4.

> Have you ever given up? Have you ever had a bad experience turn into something good?

> What kinds of activities bring people together? Have you ever signed up for any of them?

> Who do you get along with well? Do you count on those people? Do you ever feel like you have to keep up with them?

16 | Unit 2

# Grammar: Past perfect and past perfect continuous

**6. Complete the chart.**

| Past perfect continuous |
|---|
| Use the past perfect continuous for experiences that started in the past and continued up until another time in the past. |

| | |
|---|---|
| What **had** they **been doing**? They _____ cell phones before the program started. They **hadn't been using** email. | _____ they **been using** cell phones? Yes, they **had**. No, they _____. |

| Past perfect vs. past perfect continuous |
|---|
| Remember to use the past perfect to refer to something that happened before a specific time in the past. Use the past perfect to emphasize the result. |
| Fifty people **had signed** up this year.    I **hadn't heard** of that job. |
| Use the past perfect continuous to emphasize the action. |
| I _____ **working** with Helen for 6 months. |

▸ Check your answers: Grammar reference, p. 107

**7. Complete the sentences using the past perfect continuous form of the verbs.**

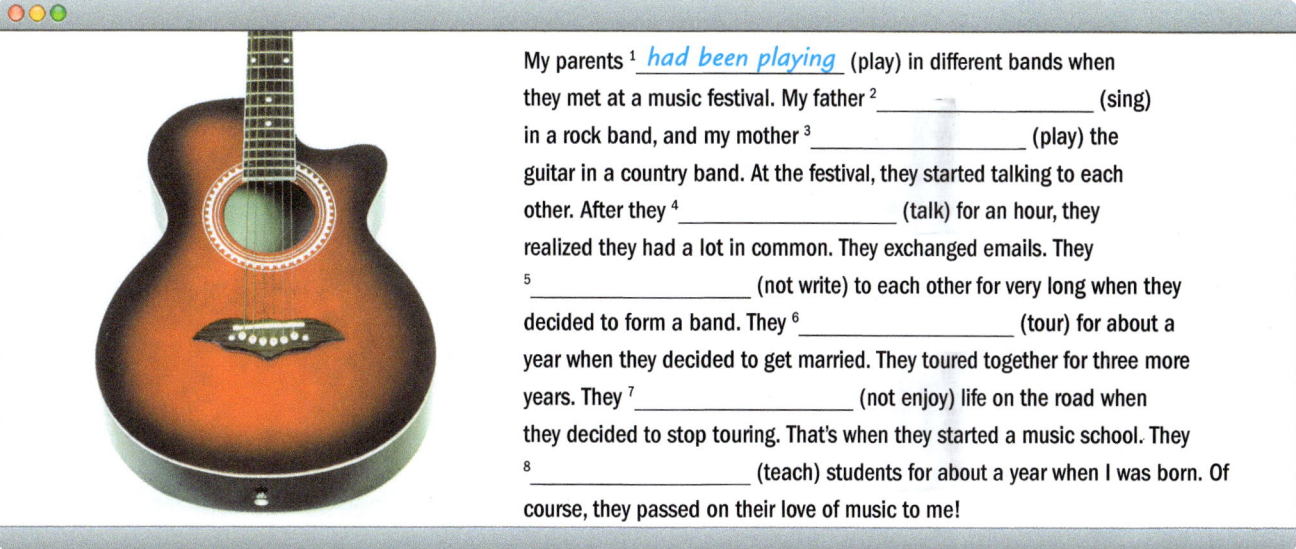

My parents ¹ *had been playing* (play) in different bands when they met at a music festival. My father ² _____ (sing) in a rock band, and my mother ³ _____ (play) the guitar in a country band. At the festival, they started talking to each other. After they ⁴ _____ (talk) for an hour, they realized they had a lot in common. They exchanged emails. They ⁵ _____ (not write) to each other for very long when they decided to form a band. They ⁶ _____ (tour) for about a year when they decided to get married. They toured together for three more years. They ⁷ _____ (not enjoy) life on the road when they decided to stop touring. That's when they started a music school. They ⁸ _____ (teach) students for about a year when I was born. Of course, they passed on their love of music to me!

**8. Complete the sentences with the past perfect continuous when possible. When not possible, use the past perfect.**

1. I *had liked* (like) music ever since I was a little kid.
2. I _____ (play) the piano for two years when my mother gave me her guitar.
3. I _____ (sign up) for classes as soon as I got my guitar.
4. I _____ (take) classes for a year when I started a band.
5. My band _____ (be) determined to make it big in music.

*Use the past perfect, not the past perfect continuous, with* ever, never, just, already, *and* yet.

I **hadn't ever heard** of that job.
(NOT: I **hadn't ever been hearing** of that job.)

*Use the past perfect, not the past perfect continuous, with* be, know, *and* like.

She **had been** a typist in the '60s.
(NOT: She **had been being** a typist in the '60s.)

## Speaking: Self-improvement

**9. YOUR TURN** Work with a partner. Talk about something you did to improve a skill or talent.

> I had been studying French before I took a Spanish class.
> I hadn't been looking for a Spanish class for very long when . . .

▸ Workbook, pp. 10–11

REAL TALK 2.2 HOW HAVE YOU HELPED A FRIEND?

# Lending an EAR

## Conversation: Finding solutions

1. **REAL TALK** Watch or listen to the teenagers talk about how they've helped people. Check (✓) the things they have helped with.

   - ☐ not making a sports team
   - ☐ the death of a pet
   - ☐ difficult situations
   - ☐ the loss of a parent's job
   - ☐ not getting a coaching job
   - ☐ getting people out of trouble
   - ☐ speaking in public
   - ☐ studying for an exam
   - ☐ buying a new pet
   - ☐ getting people into trouble
   - ☐ watching too much TV
   - ☐ finishing homework

2. **YOUR TURN** How have *you* helped a friend through a difficult situation? Tell your partner.

3. Listen to Mari tell Erica about a problem. Complete the conversation.

**USEFUL LANGUAGE: Showing concern**

✓ Are you all right?  I'm sorry to hear that.  Is there anything I can do?
I hope things get better.  What's the matter?  What's wrong with

**Erica:** Hey, Mari. ¹ _Are you all right?_
**Mari:** Well, not really.
**Erica:** ² _____
**Mari:** It's my sister.
**Erica:** ³ _____ your sister? Is she sick?
**Mari:** Oh, no, it's nothing like that. She's just really mad at me!
**Erica:** Why's that?
**Mari:** I borrowed her favorite sweater, and I ruined it.
**Erica:** ⁴ _____
**Mari:** Thanks. I feel awful about it. And now she won't even talk to me.
**Erica:** ⁵ _____
**Mari:** Yeah. Me, too.
**Erica:** ⁶ _____
**Mari:** Maybe you could go shopping with me. I'd like to buy her a new sweater.
**Erica:** That's a great idea. That should make her happy, right?
**Mari:** I think so. But maybe I'll buy her two sweaters. Then she *has to* forgive me!

4. Practice the conversation with a partner.

5. **YOUR TURN** Work with a partner. Take turns talking about a problem and showing concern. Use the problems below or your own ideas.

| Problem A | Problem B |
|---|---|
| You want to go to a concert with your friends, but your parents won't let you go. | Your brother or sister wants you to come to his/her soccer game, but you can't make it. |

18 | Unit 2

To: ted.hutchins@cup.net
From: p.hutchins03@cup.net
Subject: Thanks for your help!

Hi Grandpa,

I'm writing to thank you for listening to me and helping me with my new school. The work was harder than at my old school. I wasn't keeping up with the other students, and I'd felt like giving up. Thank you for telling me to explain the problem to my teachers. Soon, they realized I was determined to get better. Since then, they've been helping me a lot.

Making friends wasn't easy either. You know how shy I am, and it was hard to make friends. Thanks so much for your advice to smile and ask questions. Gradually, I started to feel more sociable. I've made a few good friends, and we get along really well. I had been spending a lot of time alone, but thanks to you, I'm busy with my friends all the time! I've attached a picture of me with a few of them. I really appreciate your help, Grandpa.

Thanks again,

Peter

## Reading to write: A thank-you email for support

**6.** Look at the photo. What do you think Peter is thanking his grandfather for? Read his email to check.

### Focus on CONTENT
Include these things in a thank-you email:
- a greeting
- a reason for writing
- details: Include what he/she did to help you and how it helped.
- a closing:
If you send a photo, use:
- by mail: *I've included a picture/photo of . . .*
- by email: *I've attached a picture/photo of . . .*

**7.** Read Peter's email again. What expressions from the Focus on Content box did he use? What two things did his grandfather tell him to do? How did it help?

### Focus on LANGUAGE
Use these transitional phrases to link your ideas. Use a comma after the phrases.
- happening before something: *Before that, Prior to that,*
- happening after something: *Since then, After that,*
- happening quickly after something: *Soon, Immediately,*
- happening slowly over time: *Slowly, Gradually,*

**8.** What transitional phrases does Peter use in his thank-you email?

**9.** Circle the correct answers.

1. Janice had been practicing the piano every day for a year. **Before that / Slowly**, she got better.

2. It started to rain during soccer practice. **Immediately / Gradually**, we went inside.

3. Ted's parents bought a new boat. **Slowly / After that**, he started waterskiing.

### Writing: Your thank-you email for support

◯ **PLAN**
You are going to write a thank-you email to someone for his/her support. Think of a time someone helped you. Complete the chart.

| What he/she did to help you | How it helped |
|---|---|
|  |  |
|  |  |

◯ **WRITE**
Write your thank-you email. Use your notes to help you. Include transitional phrases in your description of how the person helped you. Write at least 125 words.

◯ **CHECK**
Check your writing. Can you answer "yes" to these questions?

- Is information from the Focus on Content box in your email?
- Do you use transitional phrases correctly?

# Leaving Home to HELP

**K**wame lives in Ghana in an Ashanti village in the rainforest. He had been working in his village when he decided to leave home to go to school. He was determined to make a better life for himself. However, after he left, he realized the many good things about his home. After he finished school, he returned to his village. He wanted to make things better not only for himself, but also for his family and community. He started a school in his village. But that wasn't enough . . . he wanted to help others learn about the Ashanti people. As a child, he had learned to play the talking drum. The drum has been important to Ashanti people for many generations as a way to learn the language, communicate news, and for special ceremonies. Now, Kwame travels to schools in the cities to teach students about the talking drum and the Ashanti way of life. We spoke with Kwame to learn more.

**Q** 1 _____

**A** I'm passionate about my culture, and the talking drum is a big part of it. My uncle passed on the tradition to me, and I wanted to pass it on to others.

**Q** 2 _____

**A** I'm pretty shy, and as a result, no one was paying attention. Then I started playing the drum before I even spoke. That captured everyone's attention. The drum really does communicate. Students listen to the drum and then they want to listen to me. The drum helped me improve my presentation skills.

**Q** 3 _____

**A** Definitely how important my culture is. Also, how something as simple as a drum can bring people together. The more people understand about my culture, the more likely it is to survive. My family and community are counting on me!

## Culture: An interview with an Ashanti person

1. Look at the photos. What do you think the article is about?

2. Read the interview. Complete the interview with the questions. Then listen and check your answers.

   What's the most important thing you've learned from your experience?

   Why did you decide to teach others about the talking drum?

   What has been the hardest part about teaching others about your culture?

3. Read the interview again. Are the sentences true or false? Write *T* (true), *F* (false), or *NI* (no information).

   1. Kwame didn't like working in his village. ____
   2. He wanted to help himself more than he wanted to help his family. ____
   3. He goes to schools to teach people about his culture. ____
   4. Kwame's father taught him to play the talking drum. ____
   5. Kwame isn't shy anymore. ____

4. **YOUR TURN** Work with a partner. Do you know someone who has left home to help his or her family? Do you know someone who has helped his or her family in another way? What did they do?

### DID YOU KNOW...?

There are many types of Ashanti drums. The talking drums are called *atumpan*.

**BE CURIOUS** Find out about Sun Feng's job. What's difficult about it? (Workbook, p. 75)

Discovery EDUCATION
2.3 SHANGHAI HEIGHTS

# UNIT 2 REVIEW

## Vocabulary

**1. Complete the sentences with the correct words.**

| determined | passionate | strict |
| easy-going | shy | talented |
| impatient | sociable | |

1. Lola is extremely _____. She plays the piano well.
2. My sister is very _____. She never gives up!
3. Don is pretty _____. He gets along with everyone, but he doesn't talk very much. However, his sister is very _____. She talks to anyone!
4. My boss is very _____. We can't be late to work, and he gets so angry about the littlest things. I wish he were _____.
5. Tonya is so _____. She runs with her friends, and she gets frustrated when they can't keep up with her.
6. Barry is _____ about so many things, but he loves rock climbing the most.

## Grammar

**2. Correct the sentences.**

1. Tonya was studying dance for four years, and she's in an advanced dance class now.
2. I've been knowing Tom for 16 years.
3. Jared has took six rock-climbing trips this past year.
4. How have you been do in your art classes?
5. We used to go to summer camp, but we not having gone in years.
6. You haven't been ride your bike by my house lately.

**3. Write sentences with past perfect continuous when possible. When not possible, use the past perfect.**

1. we / have / work / for 6 hours
   _____
2. Rick / be / passionate / about photography since 2005
   _____
3. Eve and Jun / never / go / to that school
   _____
4. Anna / not study / all day
   _____
5. I / just / see / a fantastic movie
   _____

## Useful language

**4. Choose the correct answers.**

1. **A:** Are you **all right / anything**?
   **B:** No, not really. I'm having trouble in one of my classes.
   **A:** I'm sorry. I hope things get **better / matter**.
2. **A:** What's the **wrong / matter**?
   **B:** My parents won't let me go the movies.
   **A:** Is there **anything / hope** I can do?
3. **A:** What's **wrong / sorry** with Julie?
   **B:** I think her grandmother is sick.
   **A:** I'm sorry to hear **better / that**.

---

**PROGRESS CHECK: Now I can . . .**

☐ talk about a person's qualities.
☐ talk about recent events.
☐ talk about personal experiences.
☐ show concern.
☐ write a thank-you email.
☐ talk about someone who has helped his/her family.

**CLIL PROJECT**
2.4 THE HOUSE OF THE FUTURE, p. 116

# 3 Planning for the Future

### Discovery EDUCATION

**BE CURIOUS**

What a Waste!

Are you saving up for something special?

Mission: Possible?

1. What is the person doing? Where is she?

2. What do you think she is thinking about?

3. What do you think about when you think about the future?

**UNIT CONTENTS**

**Vocabulary** Verbs of the future; Achievements
**Grammar** Future review: Future continuous and future perfect
**Listening** The waters around you

## Vocabulary: Verbs of the future

**1. Match the sentences with the correct pictures.**

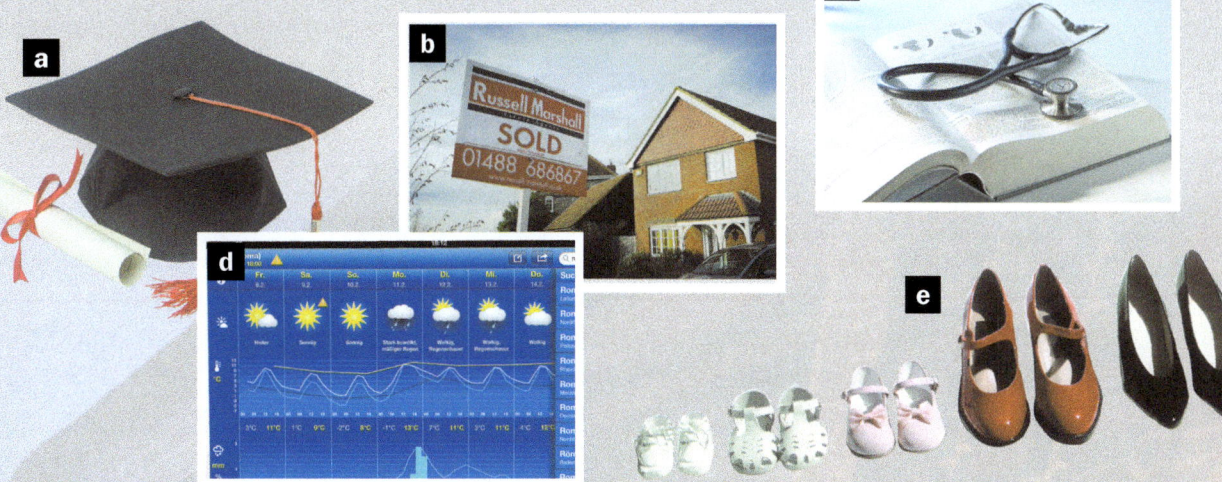

1. __e__ Children **grow up** so fast.
2. _____ If you **plan** to **become** a doctor, you have to **keep on** studying after college.
3. _____ Meteorologists try to **predict** the weather.
4. _____ Many high school students **graduate** in May.
5. _____ People often **move** to new homes because of work and **end up** in new cities.

**2. Listen, check, and repeat.**

**3. Complete the sentences with the correct verbs from Exercise 1.**

Hi, I'm Todd. I live in Jackson, Wyoming. I've lived here since I was a baby, and it was a great place to ¹ __grow up__. I'll ² _____ from high school in May. I'm really excited! I ³ _____ to go to college in the fall. I want to ⁴ _____ a computer engineer. Of course, I'll have to ⁵ _____ studying after college if I want a really good job. After that, I'll probably ⁶ _____ to California. All of the successful software designers ⁷ _____ there. I ⁸ _____ that I'll eventually come back to Jackson, but not until I'm much older, like when I retire!

## Speaking: Plans change

**4. YOUR TURN Work with a partner. Talk about someone you know who . . .**

☐ wants to move to another country in the future.
☐ wants to become a doctor when he/she grows up.
☐ plans to keep on studying after high school.
☐ plans to graduate early.

*My cousin wants to move to Argentina in a few years.*

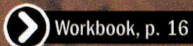
Workbook, p. 16

**Reading** A Career in Space; Leaving School Early; School in the Cloud
**Conversation** Expressing cause and effect
**Writing** An opinion essay

# A FAR AWAY FUTURE

## A CAREER IN SPACE

Are you planning to become an astronaut? Do you think you'll move to the space station one day? If so, plan to study A LOT before you graduate from space school.

David Gomez is thinking about a career in space. He is determined to become an astronaut for the National Aeronautics and Space Administration (NASA) in Houston, Texas, someday. Last year, he went to space camp and learned what it takes to be an astronaut. First, he needs to get a college degree in engineering, science, or math. Then he needs to have three years of professional experience or 1,000 hours as a pilot. Finally, he needs to pass a medical exam. If he gets into NASA's Astronaut Corps, his training will look something like this:

He will have two years of training. He'll have science and technology classes. He'll also learn medical skills. As an astronaut, he's going to need to know what to do in an emergency. He'll also learn how the International Space Station (ISS) works. He will take scuba diving courses, too. Astronauts train underwater to understand what it is like in space with no gravity. In addition, he'll take Russian classes. When he finishes training, he can be sent on a space mission. He'll learn even more on the job.

David is confident he'll get into NASA's program. He's already preparing for his future career. Next year, he's taking advanced science and math classes. He's also going to take Russian after school. After he graduates, he's going to move to Houston and go to college there.

He's extremely motivated and excited about his future career. He plans to move to the ISS someday. We predict he'll end up working for NASA and that his dream will come true!

### DID YOU KNOW...?
Astronauts who live on the ISS live there for 3 to 6 months at a time.

## Reading: An article about becoming an astronaut

1. Look at the pictures. What do you think David wants to become?

2. Read and listen to the article. What does it give information about?
   a. different careers at NASA
   b. what it takes to become an astronaut
   c. how to survive on the International Space Station

3. Read the article again. Then read the sentences and write **B** (before training), **D** (during training), or **A** (after training).
   1. Find out how the ISS works. _____
   2. Get 1,000 hours of flying experience. _____
   3. Get a college degree. _____
   4. Go on a mission. _____
   5. Learn medical skills. _____
   6. Learn to scuba dive. _____
   7. Pass a medical exam. _____
   8. Possibly live in the ISS. _____

4. **YOUR TURN** Work with a partner. Would you like to become an astronaut? Why or why not?

### Say it RIGHT!

When a word that starts with **h** links to the words before it, the **h** can be silent. Listen to the differences in these sentences.
**H** pronounced: First, **he** needs to get a college degree.
Silent **h**: Then **he** needs to have three years of professional experience.
Listen to and repeat these sentences from the article. Circle the words with pronounced **h**'s. Cross out the words with silent **h**'s.
1. If he gets into NASA's Astronaut Corps, his training will look something like this.
2. When he finishes training, he can be sent on a space mission.
3. After he graduates, he's going to move to Houston.
4. He's extremely motivated and excited about his future career.

# Grammar: Future review

**5. Complete the chart.**

| will | be going to |
|---|---|
| *Use will for predictions.* | *Use going to for planned actions and events.* |
| What classes **will** David **take**? He _____ Russian classes. He **won't take** French. | Where **is** he **going to live**? He **is going to live** in Houston. He _____ in his hometown. |
| **Present continuous** | **Simple present** |
| *Use the present continuous for planned actions and events.* | *Use the simple present for scheduled future events.* |
| What classes **is** he **taking** next year? He _____ advanced science. He **isn't taking** art classes. | Where _____ he _____ to go? He **plans** to go to the ISS. He **doesn't plan** to go to Russia. |

> Check your answers: Grammar reference, p. 108

**6. Circle the correct answers.**

Today is Aaron Lucas's first day at his dream job as a train driver, and Penn Station is his destination. The train [1]**leaves / is leaving** Boston at 1:40 p.m. and [2]**isn't arriving / arrives** about 4 hours later. Next week, he [3]**is going to drive / drives** further – from Boston to Chicago. It's a long trip! It [4]**will take / is taking** about 23 hours. The good news is that he [5]**doesn't travel / isn't traveling** alone. His family [6]**makes / is making** the trip to Chicago, too.

**7. Write sentences with the future forms given.**

1. Taylor and Joe / travel / to Colombia next year (*be going to*)
   *Taylor and Joe are going to travel to Colombia next year.*

2. cars / be / driverless in the future (*will*)
   _____

3. Martin / have / a soccer game next Friday (*simple present*)
   _____

4. I / not take / Russian next year (*present continuous*)
   _____

5. You / not like / that movie (*will*)
   _____

6. Sarah / study / science in college (*be going to*)
   _____

# Speaking: Your future – near and far

**8. YOUR TURN** Work with a partner. Talk about your future plans for the times below. How sure are you? Use *will* for predictions. Use *be going to*, the present continuous, or the simple present for planned events.

| tomorrow | next week | next year |
|---|---|---|
| in 5 years | in 10 years | |

*I'll become a chef in five years. I'm planning to take cooking classes next year.*

BE CURIOUS — Find out about e-waste. What is it? (Workbook, p. 76)

3.1 WHAT A WASTE!

# A Better FUTURE

## Listening: The waters around you

1. Do you ever swim or do sports in the ocean? What do you do? Have you ever noticed trash in the ocean?

2. Listen to a show about Dive for Debris. What does the organization do?

3. Listen again. Circle the correct answers.
    1. The divers in Dive for Debris are _____.
        a. professional divers
        b. volunteers
    2. Divers collect trash in an area _____.
        a. once
        b. many times
    3. In the future, Dive for Debris will work with _____.
        a. waste management companies
        b. local schools and teachers
    4. About _____ volunteers have collected litter in the ocean.
        a. 100
        b. 1,600

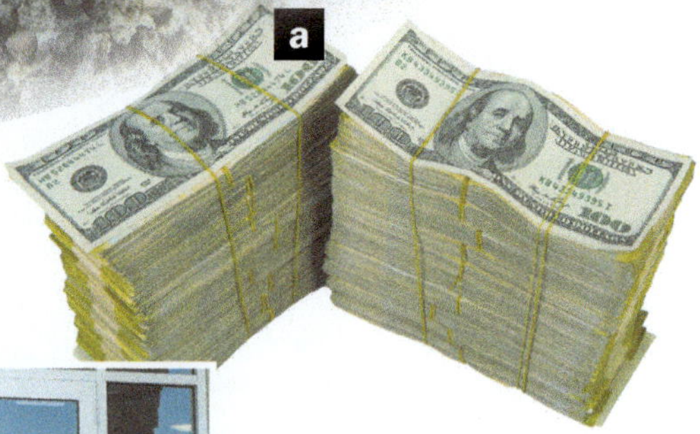

## Vocabulary: Achievements

4. Match the pictures with the correct words. Then listen, check, and repeat.
    1. _g_ become famous
    2. ___ break a record
    3. ___ develop a project
    4. ___ do volunteer work
    5. ___ make a million dollars
    6. ___ start a business
    7. ___ support the community
    8. ___ win an award

5. **YOUR TURN** Work with a partner. Rank the achievements from Exercise 4 in order of importance for you. Share your ideas with a partner and explain why.

> Doing volunteer work is number 1 for me. I think it's important because . . .

## Grammar: Future continuous and future perfect

**6. Complete the chart.**

### Future continuous

Use the future continuous to describe something that will be in progress in the future. To form the future continuous, use will + be + the -ing form of a verb.

| Who **will** be **volunteering**? Many more divers _____. I **won't be volunteering**. | _____ you **be volunteering**? Yes, I **will**. No, I _____. |
|---|---|

### Future perfect

Use the future perfect to describe something that is going to be finished at a certain time in the future. To form the future perfect, use will + have + past participle.

| How much trash **will** she **have collected** in 20 years? She _____ a lot of trash. She **won't have earned** much money. | **Will** she **have collected** a lot of trash? Yes, she _____. No, she **won't have**. |
|---|---|

> Check your answers: Grammar reference, p. 108

**7. Put the words in the correct order to complete the sentences.**

1. making / will / dollars / a / Janet's company / be / million

   <u>Janet's company will be making a million dollars</u> by 2020.

2. have / the organization / supported / will

   In 2020, _____ the community for 50 years.

3. be / Danilo / the / will / beach / cleaning up

   By this time tomorrow, _____.

4. picked up / they / have / will

   By the end of the day, _____ all of the trash?

5. will / started / company / you / have / your

   In September, _____ a year ago.

6. living / I / will / be

   _____ in Chicago in August.

> **Get it RIGHT!**
>
> Use the correct word order for questions with the future perfect.
>
> **Will** she **have** collected a lot of trash? (NOT: ~~Will have she collected a lot of trash?~~)

**8. Complete the sentences with the future continuous or future perfect.**

1. Lucy <u>will have seen</u> 20 landmarks by the time she returns from her trip.
2. In January, I _____ (know) my best friend for 15 years.
3. _____ you _____ (volunteer) at the community clean up tomorrow? We really need your help!
4. My father _____ (not work) at the community center on Saturday. He has a doctor's appointment.
5. By this afternoon, Jeremy _____ (hear) the results of his interview.
6. What _____ you _____ (do) tomorrow morning? Can you help me with something?

> **NOTICE IT**
>
> Remember, *be*, *know*, *understand*, *like*, *want*, and *need* aren't usually used in continuous forms. In addition, many sense verbs, like *feel*, *see*, and *hear* aren't usually used with the continuous.

## Speaking: Predictions for my future

**9. YOUR TURN** Work with a partner. Talk about your life in 30 years. What will you be doing? What will you have achieved?

> *In 30 years, I'll be living in Tokyo. I'll have learned Japanese, and I'll be working for a computer company. I'll . . .*

 **REAL TALK** 3.2 ARE YOU SAVING UP FOR SOMETHING SPECIAL?

# Saving for the
# FUTURE

## Conversation: Planning and budgeting

1. **REAL TALK** Watch or listen to the teenagers talk about what they are saving money for. Complete the items.

   1. concert _____
   2. an electric _____
   3. a secondhand _____
   4. _____ in two years
   5. a summer _____

2. **YOUR TURN** Are *you* saving up for something special? What? Tell your partner.

3. Listen to Nora talking with Mr. Lee about the budget for a school trip. Complete the conversation.

**USEFUL LANGUAGE: Expressing cause and effect**

as a result | consequently | because of | since | ✓so that | thanks to

**Mr. Lee:** Thanks for helping me with the budget for our school trip, Nora. Just think, this time next month, you'll be riding horses at a ranch!

**Nora:** I know! Everyone's really excited.

**Mr. Lee:** Your class has saved a lot of money for the trip [1] _so that_ students don't have to pay. But I don't think we have enough for everything we've planned. [2]_____, we're going to have to make some cuts.

**Nora:** Well, I just talked to Lauren Rigby. And [3]_____ her, the cost of horseback riding at the ranch is going to be cheaper.

**Mr. Lee:** Really? Why?

**Nora:** [4]_____ the owners are Lauren's aunt and uncle, they're going to give us a discount.

**Mr. Lee:** That's nice. So, we should have enough money for food. I'm not sure if we have enough for transportation, though. [5]_____ the number of people going, we have to rent one of the bigger buses, and they're pretty expensive.

**Nora:** What if we get parent volunteers to drive us? [6]_____, we'd save a lot of money.

**Mr. Lee:** That's a good idea, Nora.

4. Practice the conversation with a partner.

5. **YOUR TURN** Work with a partner. Have a conversation about a budget for one of the items below or your own idea.

   a school dance | a new sports center for the school | an after-school club

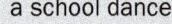

## LEAVING SCHOOL EARLY

*Should students be allowed to leave school before they are 18?*

by Rita Newman

In the United States, the school-leaving age is different from state to state, but it is usually 16 years old, meaning some students can legally leave school before their senior year. Personally, I don't think it's a good idea to make everyone stay until they are 18.

Obviously, students who want to go to college will stay in school until they are 18 anyway, but not everyone enjoys studying. Many young people would rather work or take a training course. They want to learn skills so that they will be able to get jobs.

Certainly, students who don't want to stay in school will behave badly. What's more, they will create problems for other students and teachers. It is better to allow students to leave and pursue other things.

Consequently, I'm against forcing students to stay in school, at least until schools can provide a wider range of training courses and work experience.

## Reading to write: An opinion essay

**6.** Look at the title and the photo. What do you think Rita's opinion will be? Read her essay to check.

> ◉ *Focus on* **CONTENT**
> When you write an opinion essay, organize it like this:
> - introduction (1 paragraph): Introduce the topic and state your opinion.
> - body (1 to 3 paragraphs): Give reasons for your opinion.
> - conclusion: State your opinion again.

**7.** Read Rita's essay again. What reasons does Rita give for her opinion?

> ◉ *Focus on* **LANGUAGE**
> Use adverbs to show how you feel about your opinions:
> - to show something is in your opinion: *personally*
> - to show that everyone knows it: *obviously, clearly*
> - to show it's certain to happen: *certainly, surely, definitely, inevitably*
> - to show the result of something you said: *therefore, consequently, accordingly*
> Use connecting words and phrases to add additional ideas: *in addition, what's more, also*

**8.** Which adverbs does Rita use in her essay? Which connecting phrase does she use?

**9.** Circle the correct answers.

1. **Obviously / Personally**, science is important.

2. Everyone should know how food is grown. **Therefore / What's more**, I think high school students should take a food science class.

3. Crime is a problem in this area. **In addition / Surely**, we need more police officers.

4. Teenagers should start saving money for their futures. They should **inevitably / also** start to explore career options.

## Writing: Your opinion essay

### ▢ PLAN

You are going to write an opinion essay. Choose one of the questions below and complete the chart.

- Should teenagers work before they are 16?
- Should parents give teenagers spending money?

| Question | |
|---|---|
| Your opinion | |
| Reasons for your opinion | |

### ▢ WRITE

Write your opinion essay. Use your notes to help you. Include an introduction, body, and conclusion. Use adverbs and connecting phrases. Write at least 125 words.

### ▢ CHECK

Check your writing. Can you answer "yes" to these questions?

- Is information from the Focus on Content box in your essay?
- Do you use adverbs and connecting phrases correctly?

# School in the CLOUD

What do you think school will be like in the future? In 1999, Sugata Mitra had an idea for a school of the future. He got his idea when he put a computer in a classroom full of students who had never used one before. Amazingly, the students taught themselves how to use it. To Mitra, this was not so amazing. He believed that children could teach themselves just about anything! He imagined students in a classroom with an adult who gave them questions to answer, like "Why do animals cry?" or "Why is the sky blue?" Students would be in charge of their own learning and would work together using the Internet to answer those questions.

In 2013, Mitra started such a school, called a *School in the Cloud lab*, in a high school in England. Soon after, three School in the Cloud labs opened in India.

School in the Cloud also has SOLEs – Self-Organized Learning Environments. A SOLE is similar to a lab, but it's done after school and on the weekends, and students are not in a classroom. They work together over the Internet. Any adult can start a SOLE. SOLE leaders are volunteers, and they're called *Grannies*. Their job is to help children learn. They post a question to students online, and students work however they want to find the answers. Grannies are there to encourage students and help them as they discover answers.

Mitra calls his schools a "global experiment," and he hopes to create more of them around the world. His dream is likely to come true. In 2013, he won an award to develop his project – one million dollars. He feels this money will help fund more schools that allow children to learn by discovery.

## Culture: An article about a new way of learning

1. Look at the title. What do you think School in the Cloud is?

3.08

2. Read and listen to the article. What's the article's purpose?

   a. To teach people how to start a SOLE

   b. To explain what School in the Cloud is

   c. To compare School in the Cloud to a traditional classroom

3. Read the article again. Are the sentences true or false? Write *T* (true), *F* (false), or *NI* (no information).

   1. Sugata Mitra gives teachers ideas for questions to ask students. ____

   2. The first School in the Cloud started in India. ____

   3. "Grannies" get paid to work with students. ____

   4. At School in the Cloud students can work together. ____

   5. Mitra hopes to have one million schools in the future. ____

   6. Mitra thinks students are able to learn by themselves. ____

4. **YOUR TURN** Work with a group. Imagine what school will be like in 100 years. Share your ideas.

   *I think that classrooms will be in space in 100 years. Students will learn while . . .*

### DID YOU KNOW...?
Some experts predict that about 5 billion people will be using the Internet by 2020.

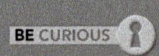  Find out about space travel. What problem do astronauts have? (Workbook, p. 77)

3.3 MISSION: POSSIBLE?

# UNIT 3 REVIEW

## Vocabulary

**1. Complete the sentences with the correct forms of words.**

| become | grow up | plan |
|---|---|---|
| ✓ end up | keep on | predict |
| graduate | move | |

1. Becky won an award on a talent show, and she _ended up_ becoming famous.
2. I need to _____ studying after high school if I want to start a business.
3. After _____ to New York City, I immediately started doing volunteer work.
4. I _____ to study math in college.
5. My sister will have _____ from high school by the time I start middle school.
6. Why do you want to _____ an astronaut?
7. I _____ that I will break a record at the race tomorrow.
8. Do you want to become famous when you _____?

## Grammar

**2. Rewrite the sentences. Use the future forms given.**

1. I'm doing volunteer work on Saturday. (be going to)

   _I'm going to do volunteer work on Saturday._

2. I'm planning on making a million dollars someday. (will)

   _____

3. Josh isn't going to work after school next week. (present continuous)

   _____

4. What time does the train leave on Monday? (be going to)

   _____

5. The party will start at 10:00 a.m. on Friday. (simple present)

   _____

6. He isn't going to be an astronaut when he grows up. (will)

   _____

**3. Correct the future continuous and future perfect mistakes in the sentences.**

1. Lyle will have ~~saving~~ _saved_ $1,000 by September.
2. Have you be diving with the group on Sunday?
3. Gina and Tom will be save money after they get jobs.
4. How many years won't she have flown before she goes on the space shuttle?
5. Mary won't be lived in Denver long by the time I move there.
6. I won't attending Carl's graduation party next weekend.

## Useful language

**4. Complete the sentences with the correct words.**

1. Vicky is sick. C_____, she can't go to space camp.
2. We don't have to pay for our class trip b_____ _____ a donation from a business.
3. I'm saving up my money s_____ t_____ I can buy a bicycle.
4. The bus broke down this morning. A_____ a r_____, Caleb was late to work.
5. We applied to the program early s_____ it usually fills up fast.
6. T_____ _____ my aunt, I have a summer job.

---

**PROGRESS CHECK: Now I can . . .**

☐ talk about people's plans for the future.
☐ talk about my plans for the near and distant future.
☐ make predictions about the future.
☐ express cause and effect.
☐ write an opinion essay.
☐ discuss what schools will be like in the future.

## Vocabulary: Cooking verbs

**1. Label the pictures with the correct words.**

bake   boil   chop   fry   grate   grill   mix   ✓roast   slice

1. __roast__    2.  _____   3.  _____   4.  _____   5. _____

6.  _____   7.  _____   8.  _____   9. _____

**2. Listen, check, and repeat.**

🔊 4.01

**3. Work with a partner. What can you do with these foods? Check (✓) the correct columns and then discuss.**

|  | bake, fry, roast, and grill | boil | chop | mix | slice |
|---|---|---|---|---|---|
| 1. chicken |  |  |  |  |  |
| 2. cheese |  |  |  |  |  |
| 3. onions |  |  |  |  |  |
| 4. spices |  |  |  |  |  |
| 5. strawberries |  |  |  |  |  |

> You can bake, fry, roast, and grill chicken.
>
> You can also boil it and then use it to make chicken salad.

**NOTICE IT**
*bake* = to cook something in an oven
*roast* = to cook something in an oven on high heat so it turns brown on top
*chop* = to cut something into small pieces
*slice* = to cut something into thin, flat pieces

## Speaking: A good recipe

**4. YOUR TURN Choose a simple recipe you know. Write the steps. Add as many steps as you need.**

First, . . . → Then . . . → Next, . . . → Finally, . . .

_First, fry the beef._ _____

_Then grate cheese and . . ._ _____

**5. Work with a partner. Tell your partner how to make your recipe.**

> Nachos are easy to make. First, fry some beef. Then grate cheese and chop onions and peppers while the beef is frying. Next, . . .

▶ Workbook, p. 22

**Reading** Food for Thought; A Traditional Dish; Pots and Pans of the Past
**Conversation** Cooking instructions
**Writing** An article about a family dish

# DANGEROUS Foods?

## FOOD FOR THOUGHT

What do you want to know about food? Ask our experts.

**Why does chopping onions make you cry? Are they dangerous?**

A poisonous gas comes out of an onion when you cut or fry it. If the gas gets into your eyes, your body makes tears to wash it out. So, the next time you chop an onion, do it under running water. When you cut an onion under running water, the gas won't get into your eyes.

**I heard fugu is poisonous. Can people eat it?**

Fugu is the world's most poisonous fish, but you can eat it! It's a very expensive fish, and it's popular in Japan. The fish has some very poisonous parts, but you can eat the rest of it. Specially trained fugu chefs learn how to slice the fish very carefully to get rid of the poisonous parts. If you are ever in Japan and want to try fugu fish, you'll have to be very careful. You'll have to go to a restaurant with a fugu-trained chef, unless you want it to be your last meal!

**Can garlic get rid of evil?**

According to legend, garlic can protect people from vampires. Of course, vampires are only in the movies, but garlic can protect us from other things. For example, mosquitos find their victims by smell. And they don't like the smell of garlic! When you eat garlic, the smell comes through your skin. If your skin smells like garlic, a mosquito probably won't bite you!

**Why are so many people allergic to peanuts?**

Peanut oil contains a chemical called *glycerol*, which can be used to make dynamite. Many people are allergic to glycerol. They get sick, have trouble breathing, or get a rash after eating food with glycerol in it. Many dogs are allergic to peanuts, too! Even the smallest piece of peanut can cause serious problems for people or animals with peanut allergies. You'll need to get to a hospital immediately if you have an allergic reaction to a peanut.

## Reading: An article about dangerous foods

1. **Look at the pictures. What foods do you see?**

2. **Read and listen to the article. What bad things are mentioned about the foods? What good thing is mentioned about one of the foods?**

**DID YOU KNOW...?** Eating a lot of onions can make you sleepy. If you have problems sleeping, have some onion soup for dinner!

3. **Read the article again. What advice does the website give for . . .**

   1. chopping onions? _____
   2. eating peanuts if you're allergic? _____
   3. eating fugu fish? _____
   4. avoiding mosquito bites? _____

4. **YOUR TURN Work with a partner. Answer the questions.**

   1. Are you allergic to any foods? Which ones?
   2. Would you try fugu fish? Why or why not?
   3. What other dangerous foods do you know about?

# Grammar: First conditional review; zero conditional

**5. Complete the chart.**

> Use the first conditional to show results or possible results of future actions. Use *if*, *when*, or *unless* and the simple present in the main clause. Use *will (not)* and the base form of a verb in the result clause.

> **If** your skin **smells** like garlic, a mosquito probably **won't bite** you!
> You**'ll have to go** to a restaurant with a fugu-trained chef, **unless** you _____ it to be your last meal!

> Use the zero conditional to show a result of an action that is always true. Use *if*, *when*, or *unless* and the simple present in the main clause and the simple present in the result clause.

> A poisonous gas **comes** out of an onion **when** you _____ or **fry** it.
> **If** the gas **gets** into your eyes, your body _____ tears to wash it out.

> Check your answers: Grammar reference, p. 109

**6. Circle the correct answers.**

1. I never eat fish because when I (**eat**) / **will eat** it, I **get** / **will get** really sick.
2. I hope we don't get grasshoppers this year. If grasshoppers **attack** / **will attack** our crops, they **destroyed** / **will destroy** the food.
3. You **get** / **will get** a lot of mosquito bites unless you **put** / **will put** on some bug spray.
4. I **don't try** / **won't try** sushi when I **go** / **will go** to Japan next week.
5. My mom **uses** / **will use** a lot of garlic when she **cooks** / **will cook** pasta on Sundays.
6. Your breath **smells** / **will smell** if you **eat** / **will eat** that garlic bread.

### Get it RIGHT!

When talking about the future, use the simple present in the main clause with *if*, *when*, and *unless*. Do not use *will*.
If your skin **smells** like garlic, a mosquito won't bite you. (NOT: If your skin **will smell** like garlic, a mosquito won't bite you.)

**7. Write zero or first conditional sentences.**

1. if / Jackie / drink / coffee tonight ➔ not sleep well
   *If Jackie drinks coffee tonight, she won't sleep well.*

2. when / we / grill / steaks ➔ we usually / put / a lot of salt on the meat
   _____

3. Johnny / not eat / those vegetables ➔ unless / you / put / butter on them
   _____

4. I always / get / a rash ➔ if / I / eat / strawberries
   _____

5. when / water / reach / 32° ➔ it / boil
   _____

6. I / eat / chicken ➔ unless / it / be / fried
   _____

# Speaking: Party time!

**8. YOUR TURN Work with a partner. Talk about what makes a party good and bad.**

> I like parties with music!

>> Not me. It's hard to talk when there's music.
>> I like parties with interesting food.

>>> Me, too. But only if the food isn't spicy.
>>> If the food is too spicy, I don't eat it.

Workbook, pp. 22–23

**BE CURIOUS** Find out about argan oil. What is it used for? (Workbook, p. 78)

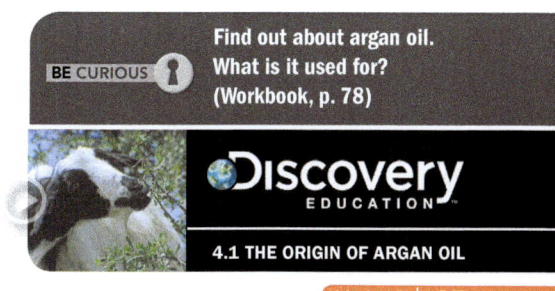

Discovery EDUCATION
4.1 THE ORIGIN OF ARGAN OIL

# Unusual FOODS

## Listening: A taste test

1. Do you like to try new foods? Why or why not?

2. Listen to three teens taking a taste test. Check (✓) the foods they try.

3. Listen again. Did the teens like the food? Complete the chart with *Yes* or *No*.

a ☐ jellyfish
b ☐ swordfish 
c ☐ fried chicken 
d ☐ fried alligator tail 
e ☐ chapulines/grasshoppers 
f ☐ beef tacos 

|  | Dale | Josie | Kristen |
|---|---|---|---|
| Food 1 | Yes |  |  |
| Food 2 |  |  |  |
| Food 3 |  |  |  |

## Vocabulary: Adjectives describing foods

4. Match the definitions (a–j) with the adjectives in sentences 1–10. Then listen and check.

1. __j__ I don't eat cookies. I prefer **savory** snacks, like nuts and chips.
2. ____ These strawberries are **delicious**! I love them!
3. ____ Quick, give me some water! This sauce is really **spicy**!
4. ____ This meal is totally **disgusting**! I hate it.
5. ____ Did you forget to put spices on the meat? It tastes very **bland**.
6. ____ Wow! This cake is very **sweet**!
7. ____ This lemonade is very **sour**. It needs more sugar.
8. ____ Yuck! This coffee doesn't have any sugar in it. It's really **bitter**.
9. ____ Have you tried these apples? They're so **crunchy**!
10. ____ I can't eat this soup because it's too **salty**!

a. having a lot of sugar
b. hard and makes a sound when you eat it
c. tasting or looking terrible
d. tasting very good
e. having a lot of salt
f. having an acid-like taste
g. strong flavor; the opposite of sweet
h. having strong spices that cause a burning feeling in your mouth
i. not having a strong flavor
j. spicy or salty and not sweet

5. **YOUR TURN** Work with a partner. Name foods that the adjectives in Exercise 4 describe. Do you like them?

> *Lemons are sour. I don't like lemons, but I like lemonade.*

> *I like lemons on grilled fish. It's a savory dish.*

# Grammar: Second conditional review

**6. Complete the chart.**

*Use the second conditional to describe imaginary situations and possible consequences. Use if or unless + simple past for the imaginary situation. Use would (not) + base form of the verb for the possible consequence.*

| Yes/No questions |
|---|
| **Would** you **eat** it again **if** you **had** the chance?<br>Yes, I _____. / No, I **wouldn't**.<br>**If I saw** it on a menu, I **would eat** it again.<br>I **wouldn't eat** it again _____ you **paid** me. |
| **Wh- questions** |
| **If** I **wanted** to eat *chapulines* again, where _____ I **get** them?<br>You probably **wouldn't find** them **unless** you **went** to Mexico. |

*For be, use was or were after I.*

I'd try *chapulines* if I _____ in Mexico. If
I **were** in Mexico, I'd try *chapulines*.

> Check your answers: Grammar reference, p. 109

**7. Circle the correct answers.**

1. Rafa **didn't eat** / (**wouldn't eat**) snake unless he (**was**) / **would be** very hungry!
2. **Did** / **Would** you try jellyfish if you **got** / **would get** the chance?
3. If Laura **had** / **would have** to choose between giving up chocolate or pizza, she **gave up** / **would give up** chocolate!
4. If I **were** / **would be** a fugu chef, I **were** / **would be** very worried about poisoning my customers!
5. Unless I **picked** / **would pick** them myself, I **ate** / **wouldn't eat** wild mushrooms. They could be poisonous!
6. If someone **offered** / **would offer** you an unusual food, what you **would** / **did** you do?

### NOTICE IT
*Was* and *Were* are both possible after *I* in the second conditional. *Was* is informal and *were* is more formal in style.
*If I **was** alone on an island, I'd . . .*
*If I **were** alone on an island, I'd . . .*

**8. Match the beginnings of the sentences in the zero, first, and second conditional to their endings.**

1. When I make eggs, *e*
2. If I go to Japan, ___
3. If I tried catfish, ___
4. I wouldn't eat raw fish ___
5. I'll order fish tacos ___
6. I always use beef ___

a. if I go to a Mexican restaurant.
b. I would probably like it.
c. when I make nachos.
d. unless it were sushi.
e. I boil them until they're hard.
f. I'll eat sushi.

# Speaking: Food talk

**9. YOUR TURN** Work with a partner. Ask and answer the questions.

1. If you had dinner with a famous person, who would you eat with? Why? What would you eat?
2. What foods wouldn't you eat unless you had no other choice?
3. If you were to eat only one food for the rest of your life, what would it be?

> If you had dinner with a famous person, who would you eat with?
>> I'd eat with Demi Lovato because . . .

### Say it RIGHT!
Listen to the questions. Notice the stress on the <u>word after the verb</u> in the **If** clause. Notice the stress <u>on the verb</u> in the clause asking about the possible consequence.
*If you had **dinner** with a famous person, who would you **eat** with?*
*What food would you **eat** if you were **alone** on an island?*
Practice correct stress and intonation in the questions in Exercise 9.

**REAL TALK** 4.2 WHAT WOULD YOU MAKE IF YOU HAD TO COOK FOR YOUR FAMILY?

# Family RECIPES

## Conversation: It's a one-pot meal!

1. **REAL TALK** Watch or listen to the teenagers talk about what they would cook for their families. Complete the phrases they say.

   1. steak and _____ a big green _____
   2. pasta and _____
   3. a _____ steak
   4. do the grocery _____
   5. I'd _____ breakfast. _____ and pizza
   6. _____ on the side

2. **YOUR TURN** What would *you* make if you had to cook for your family for a day? Tell your partner.

3. Listen to Josh getting cooking instructions from his mom. Complete the conversation.

**USEFUL LANGUAGE: Cooking instructions**

| a pinch of | ✓ first of all | let it simmer |
| pour it into | stir it for | then add |

**Mom:** Hi, Josh. I'm going to be home late. I need you to make dinner.
**Josh:** Really?
**Mom:** Yes. We're having spaghetti. It's so easy – it's a one-pot meal!
**Josh:** Um, OK. What do I do?
**Mom:** ¹ *First of all*, put the beef in a pan and fry it. While you're frying the beef, chop an onion and some garlic.
**Josh:** OK.
**Mom:** ² _____ the onion and garlic to the beef, and fry it for a few more minutes.
**Josh:** OK. What's next?
**Mom:** Open a can of tomato sauce, and ³ _____ the pan.
**Josh:** OK. Do I need to mix it together?
**Mom:** Of course! ⁴ _____ a couple of seconds.
**Josh:** Do I need to add any spices?
**Mom:** Yes. Add ⁵ _____ salt and a little pepper.
**Josh:** Great. And that's it?
**Mom:** Yes. Just ⁶ _____ until I get home. You know, cook it just a little . . . not a full boil. Then we'll cook the pasta when I get home.
**Josh:** OK, mom, but that's another pot – spaghetti is a two-pot meal!
**Mom:** Oh, Josh! It's still easy!

4. Practice the conversation with a partner.

5. **YOUR TURN** Work with a partner. Take turns giving cooking instructions. Use the recipe for vegetable stir fry or your own ideas.

## VEGETABLE STIR FRY

1. Cut vegetables.
2. Heat oil in a pan on very high.
3. Put vegetables into the pan.
3. Stir it for 5 to 10 minutes.
4. Pour soy sauce over the vegetables.
5. Add pepper and a pinch of salt.
6. Stir and fry for 2 more minutes.

# A TRADITIONAL DISH
*posted by Allison Bently*

I live in Ironwood, Michigan, in the United States. We have a great deal of delicious food, but our most famous dish is the pasty. To make a pasty, put enough meat and vegetables on the dough to fill it, and fold it over so it looks like the letter D. Then bake it.

Pasties are usually served hot and are easy to eat with your hands. Traditional pasties are filled with beef, potatoes, onions, and carrots, but today, they're also made with chicken. There's even a taco pasty and a pizza pasty!

Pasties came from Cornwall, England. In the 1850s, British miners came to work in Ironwood. They introduced pasties. The miners left a long time ago, but the pasties stayed. Now, it's such a traditional food in my town. You can eat pasties all over England, but in the United States, you can only find them in a few places, like Ironwood!

## Reading to write: An article about a local dish

**6.** Look at the photo. What dish do you think Allison is writing about? What's in it? Read her article to check.

> **Focus on CONTENT**
> When you write about a local dish, include these things:
> - the name of the dish
> - the main ingredients
> - how it's made
> - variations
> - how it's eaten
> - the history of the dish

**7.** Read Allison's article again. What information did she give for each item in the Focus on Content box?

> **Focus on LANGUAGE**
> Use these words to describe amounts or degrees of something without using numbers:
> *a lot of / a great deal of*: There are **a lot of** vegetables in stir fries.
> *not much, too much*: There's **not much** salt in this chicken dish, but there's **too much** pepper.
> *(not) enough*: Be sure to put **enough** pepper in the soup.
> *such, so*: This is **such** a good dish! It's **so** delicious.

**8.** Which words from the Focus on Language box does Allison use in her article?

**9.** Circle the correct answers.
1. There aren't **enough / too much** spices in this dish.
2. This soup is **such / so** salty!
3. There's **a great deal of / much** cheese in the lasagna.
4. There's **so / too much** salt on this chicken.
5. This is **such / much** a good cookie recipe.

### Writing: An article about a family dish

**PLAN**
Choose a dish that is a specialty in your family. Complete the chart.

| | |
|---|---|
| The name of the dish | |
| The main ingredients | |
| How it's made | |
| Variations | |
| How it's eaten | |
| The history of the dish | |

**WRITE**
Write an article about your dish. Use your notes to help you. Write at least 125 words.

**CHECK**
Check your writing. Can you answer "yes" to these questions?
- Is information from the Focus on Content box in your article?
- Do you use words to describe amounts or degrees of things correctly?

# Pots and Pans of the PAST

### THE MOROCCAN TAGINE

A traditional tagine is made of clay or ceramic. The bottom of the pot is wide and circular. The top is triangular. People in Morocco and other North African countries have used the tagine for hundreds of years to make meat or vegetable stews. The ingredients are chopped and put into the tagine. In the past, the tagine was put on very hot coals. Today, it is often used on top of the stove. After the stew simmers for hours, it is served in the tagine. Traditionally, everyone at the table shares this one-pot meal, eating from the tagine with bread instead of forks.

### A MĀORI HĀNGI

A long time ago, the Māori people in New Zealand didn't have any pots for cooking. They roasted, baked, and grilled food on an open fire. They also created a way to cook with steam called *hāngi*. First, they put stones in a fire. Then they dug a big hole in the ground and prepared the food – fish or chicken, potatoes, and vegetables. When the stones were hot, they put them in the hole. Cabbage leaves were put on top of the hot stones and a great deal of water was poured over it. Then the food was put on top of the cabbage, and a wet cloth was put over the food. The steam from the water cooked the food. Today, people still use this method of cooking for special feasts. However, they often put the food in metal baskets.

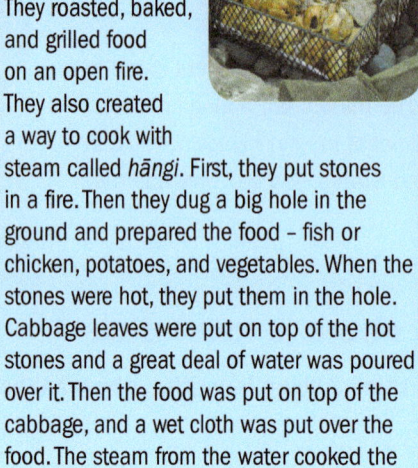

### THE MAYA MORTAR AND PESTLE

You may think that traditional foods of long ago were bland, but that's not true. Many cultures used spices thousands of years ago. Many native people of Mexico ate spicy foods. Groups like the Maya used a mortar and pestle to grind spices. The mortar is a small bowl and the pestle is a thick stick. In the past, they were made from basalt – a type of black rock. Today, some mortar and pestles are made from basalt, but they're also made from metal, ceramic, and wood. The spices go in the mortar, and they are ground with the pestle. This technology is thousands of years old, but people continue to use it in their kitchens today.

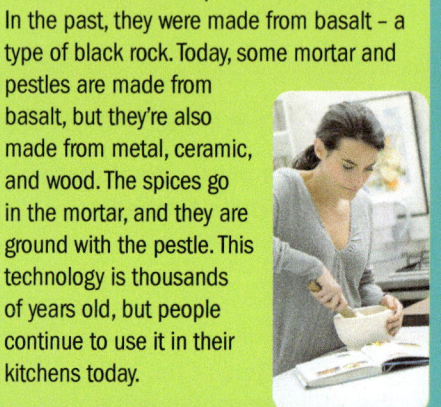

## Culture: An article about traditional cooking

1. **Look at the photos. What foods do you see?**

2. **Read and listen to the article. Match each item with its description and its use.**

   1. tagine ____ ____
   2. hāngi ____ ____
   3. mortar and pestle ____ ____

   a. used to steam food
   b. used to grind spices
   c. pot to put on a fire
   d. a bowl and a stick
   e. method of cooking in the ground
   f. used to make stews

3. **Read the article again. Write *T* (tagine), *H* (hāngi), or *M* (mortar and pestle).**

   1. The food is cooked and served in the same pot. ____
   2. It can be made from ceramic. ____ ____
   3. It has two parts. ____ ____
   4. No pots or bowls are used for cooking. ____ ____
   5. It's used to heat up food. ____ ____

4. **YOUR TURN** Work with a partner. What other traditional ways of cooking do you know?

### DID YOU KNOW...?

Archaeologists have found pots in Japan that are about 15,000 years old. They think the pots were used to cook fish.

**BE CURIOUS** Find out about fish in Japan. What are some of the kinds of seafood that people in Japan eat? (Workbook, p. 79)

**Discovery EDUCATION**

4.3 FRUITS OF THE SEA

40 | Unit 4

# UNIT 4 REVIEW

## Vocabulary

**1. Circle the correct answers.**

**Spicy Chili**

First of all, ¹**fry / slice** beef in a pan. ²**Boil / Chop** an onion and add it to the pan with the beef. Add a can of tomatoes and a cup of water. Add some pepper and a pinch of salt. Don't make it too ³**sour / salty**. Add other spices so that it's not ⁴**bland / spicy**. ⁵**Slice / Mix** it together. Let it ⁶**boil / grill** for 10 minutes and then simmer for 30 minutes. Put the chili in a bowl when it's done. ⁷**Grate / Mix** cheese and put it on top of the chili. Mmm . . . it's ⁸**disgusting / delicious**!

## Grammar

**2. Complete the sentences with the correct form of the words.**

1. If you fry garlic, it _____ (release) the flavor.
2. I _____ (go) to a Hāngi if I go to New Zealand.
3. Larry _____ (not buy) a tagine unless it's on sale.
4. If it _____ (rain), we won't eat outside.
5. Meat cooks when it _____ (be) on top of hot stones.
6. If I make pasta, I _____ (invite) you over for dinner.

**3. Write second conditional sentences and questions.**

1. if / I / have / time ➔ I / make / dinner tonight / .
   _____

2. Carlos / take / cooking classes ➔ if / he / have / enough money / .
   _____

3. I / not eat / dessert ➔ unless / it / be / chocolate / .
   _____

4. if / Janet / be / really hungry ➔ she / get / fast food / .
   _____

5. you / make / the food ➔ if / you / have / a party / ?
   _____

6. if / you / buy / a mortar and pestle ➔ where / you / buy / it / ?
   _____

## Useful language

**4. Put the phrases in the correct order in the correct sentences.**

| of / a / pinch | all / of / first | simmer / it / let |
| add / then | it / for / stir | into / pour / it |

1. This recipe only calls for _____ salt.
2. After the stew comes to a boil, _____ for an hour.
3. _____ , chop the vegetables. Next, grate the cheese.
4. Measure a cup of water and _____ the pot.
5. Fry the chicken in a pan. _____ spices.
6. Put the fruit in a bowl with juice and _____ a minute.

---

**PROGRESS CHECK: Now I can . . .**

- ☐ talk about how to prepare a simple dish.
- ☐ talk about party preferences.
- ☐ discuss imaginary situations in the future.
- ☐ give instructions for cooking.
- ☐ write about a family dish.
- ☐ talk about traditional ways of cooking.

**CLIL PROJECT**

4.4 YOU ARE WHAT YOU EAT, p. 117

# 5 Fame and Fortune

**Discovery EDUCATION**

**BE CURIOUS**

- A Cool Experiment
- How do you prepare for a sports event?
- Trendsetters

1. Who do you think the photographers are taking pictures of?

2. Do famous people walk on red carpets in your country? For what events?

3. If you were famous, what would you like to be famous for?

## UNIT CONTENTS

**Vocabulary** Verbs expressing opinions; Adverbs of degree
**Grammar** Defining and non-defining relative clauses; Tag questions
**Listening** I see your point, but . . .

## Vocabulary: Verbs expressing opinion

**1. Circle the correct answers.**

**Meet Cathy, a very opinionated person!**

*I have opinions about everything! Here's what I think about fame.*

1. I **admire** / dislike Will Smith. He's a successful actor and he works very hard.
2. I **recommend** / **hate** his movie Men in Black. It's excellent, and you can rent it online.
3. I **respect** / **feel** that celebrities should be good role models. Kids really pay attention to what they do.
4. I **prefer** / **appreciate** all the hard work that actors do. I took an acting class, and it's harder than it seems!
5. I **admire** / **prefer** movies to television shows. They're more exciting.
6. I **dislike** / **recommend** TV shows about celebrity gossip. I don't care about stars' personal lives.
7. I **hate** / **feel** reality shows! I don't know why they're popular.
8. I **respect** / **think** good actors, so I don't think reality stars should be famous when they can't act.
9. I **appreciate** / **think** acting is a wonderful job, but I want to be a director someday!

**2. Listen, check, and repeat.**

## Speaking: Movies and Music

**3. YOUR TURN** Work with a partner. Give your opinion about one of these topics.

| Movies and actors | Music and musicians |
|---|---|
| What movies do you recommend? | Are there any songs you hate? Why? |
| What do you like and dislike about going to the movies? | What singer do you admire? Why? |
| What actor do you respect? Why? | Do you feel that singers should be good role models? Why or why not? |

*I recommend Avatar. It's such a great movie. I prefer watching it on a big screen, but you can watch it on your computer. In fact, I feel like watching it right now!*

### NOTICE IT
**Feel** and **think** are often followed by **that** to express an opinion, but **that** is optional.
I **feel/think that** movie actors are better than TV actors.
I **feel/think** movie actors are better than TV actors.
**Feel** can often be followed by other expressions, such as **like** and **as if**.
I **feel like** watching a movie. = This is what I want to do.
I **feel as if** you're not listening to me. = It seems to me that you're not listening to me.

Workbook, p. 30

**Reading** Celebrity Causes; The Book Is Better!; Getting Paid for Your Opinions
**Conversation** Making a point
**Writing** A comparison/contrast essay

# Star POWER

Many celebrities do more than sing, dance, act, or play sports. A lot of people with star power give time and money to causes they care about.

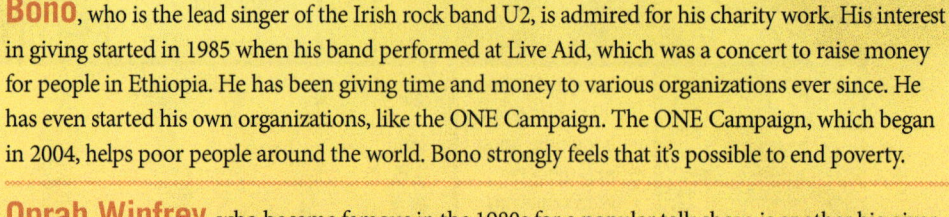

**Bono**, who is the lead singer of the Irish rock band U2, is admired for his charity work. His interest in giving started in 1985 when his band performed at Live Aid, which was a concert to raise money for people in Ethiopia. He has been giving time and money to various organizations ever since. He has even started his own organizations, like the ONE Campaign. The ONE Campaign, which began in 2004, helps poor people around the world. Bono strongly feels that it's possible to end poverty.

**Oprah Winfrey**, who became famous in the 1980s for a popular talk show, is another big giver when it comes to causes. People around the world appreciate Oprah for her generosity. The Angel Network, which Oprah started in 1998, has raised more than $50,000,000. Some of the money helped people whose homes had been ruined in Hurricane Katrina in the United States in 2005. A lot of the money was used for a girls' school in South Africa. Oprah passionately feels that everyone deserves a good education.

Sometimes, celebrities work together for a cause. During the 2014 Winter Olympics, over 100 **Olympic athletes** worked together to fight global warming. They saw the effects of global warming firsthand in Sochi, Russia, where the Olympics took place. The warmer weather affected the snow for skiing and snowboarding events. The athletes asked world leaders to do more to stop global warming.

Celebrities that give money to organizations often help bring attention to important causes. As a result, other people, who might not have known about the causes, care about them, too.

## Reading: An article about celebrity causes

1. **Look at the pictures. What causes do you think the people care about?**

2. **Read and listen to the article. Match the people with the correct causes.**

   1. Bono ___
   2. Oprah ___ ___
   3. Olympic athletes ___

   a. helping hurricane survivors
   b. global warming
   c. ending poverty
   d. education

3. **Read the article again. Are the sentences true or false? Write T (true), F (false), or NI (no information).**

   1. Bono prefers singing to doing charity work. ___
   2. The ONE Campaign helps people in Ethiopia. ___
   3. Oprah's Angel Network only helps people in natural disasters. ___
   4. All of the girls at Oprah's school in South Africa do well in class. ___
   5. Olympic athletes have not noticed global warming over the years. ___
   6. People often become interested in causes that celebrities are involved with. ___

4. **YOUR TURN** Work with a partner. Do you think celebrities should use their fame to support causes and start organizations? Why or why not?

## Grammar: Defining and non-defining relative clauses

**5. Complete the chart.**

> Use defining relative clauses with **who, which, that, where,** and **whose** to give necessary information about a noun. The sentence has a different meaning without the clause.

People _____ **make clothing** should be treated fairly.
Celebrities **that give money to organizations** often help bring attention to important causes.
Some of the money went to help people _____ **homes had been ruined**.

> Use non-defining relative clauses with **who, which, where,** and **whose** to give additional information about a noun. The clause can be left out of the sentence and it still makes sense.

Bono, _____ **is the lead singer of U2**, is admired for his charity work.
The Angel Network, **which Oprah started in 1998**, has raised more than $50,000,000.
They saw the effects of global warming in Sochi, _____ **the Olympics took place**.

> Check your answers: Grammar reference, p. 110

**6. Circle the correct answers.**

I hate reality TV stars ¹(**who**) / **whose** don't have any talent. I never watch the shows ²**which** / **where** have people living together. I do like reality shows ³**that** / **whose** are talent competitions. There were auditions for a singing competition show ⁴**that** / **where** I live. I have a cousin ⁵**which** / **who** tried out for the show, and he made it! Watch him on TV next week. He's the singer ⁶**whose** / **that** voice sounds like Elvis Presley!

**7. Combine the sentences. Make the second sentence a non-defining relative clause with who, which, where, or whose.**

1. Lilly gave money to the ONE Campaign. She likes Bono's music.
   *Lilly, who likes Bono's music, gave money to the ONE Campaign.*

2. The city of Sochi is warmer than it used to be. The 2014 Winter Olympics took place in Sochi.
   _____

3. Brad Pitt is a famous actor. His Make It Right organization helped hurricane survivors.
   _____

4. *Reality Gossip* is my favorite TV show. I watch it five nights a week.
   _____

5. We've lived in Hollywood for two years. Many celebrities live there.
   _____

### Get it RIGHT!

Don't repeat the subject in a relative clause.
Lilly, **who likes Bono's music**, gave money to the ONE campaign. (NOT: Lilly, **who ~~she~~ likes Bono's music**, gave . . . .)
Don't repeat a direct object in a relative clause.
My cousins gave money, **which they raised in two weeks**, to a charity. (NOT: My cousins gave money, **which they raised ~~it~~ in two weeks**, to a charity.)

## Speaking: Who would you help?

**8. YOUR TURN** Work with a partner. If you were a celebrity, which organization would you most want to help? Why? Discuss your ideas using relative clauses.

| an organization that helps . . . | | |
|---|---|---|
| wild animals | people in poverty | people get jobs |
| sick people | stop global warming | educate children |

> *I'd want to help an organization that helps wild animals. My cousin, who has traveled to Asia, told me that tigers are in danger.*

**BE CURIOUS** Find out about global warming. Why is Eric Gustafson doing an experiment? (Workbook, p. 80)

Discovery EDUCATION
5.1 A COOL EXPERIMENT

Workbook, pp. 30–31

Unit 5 | 45

# Making MILLIONS

## Listening: I see your point, but . . .

1. Do you ever disagree with a friend's opinion? What do you do when you disagree?

2. Listen to Jack and Mae disagree about a topic. Who thinks actors and athletes make too much money?

3. Listen again. Are the sentences true (T) or false (F)?

   1. Mae and Jack liked the movie. ____
   2. The main actor in the movie isn't very popular. ____
   3. Mae thinks that movie tickets are too expensive. ____
   4. Jack thinks that Lionel Messi only makes money for playing soccer. ____
   5. Jack feels that players should get a lot of money because they could get hurt. ____
   6. Mae and Jack don't agree on anything. ____

## Vocabulary: Adverbs of degree

4. Read the sentences and circle the sentence that is true for each situation. Then listen and check.

   1. Josh went to bed at 3:00 a.m. and got up at 6:00 a.m. He **hardly** slept at all.
      a. He didn't sleep much.    b. He slept a lot.

   2. Sandra makes $10 an hour. Vicky makes $11 an hour. Vicky makes **slightly** more money than Sandra.
      a. Vicky makes a little bit more.    b. Vicky makes a lot more.

   3. When I got home, **nearly** all of the lights were on.
      a. None of the lights were on.    b. Most of the lights were on.

   4. Laura was **pretty** excited to see her favorite singer at the concert.
      a. She was excited.    b. She wasn't excited at all.

   5. Martin, who is on two different soccer teams, is a **fairly** good player.
      a. He is good at soccer.    b. He isn't good at soccer.

   6. I saw an **absolutely** amazing movie, which my favorite actor was in.
      a. It was very good.    b. It was almost good.

   7. Usain Bolt, who has won many Olympic races, is an **extremely** fast runner.
      a. He's kind of fast.    b. He's very fast.

   8. Those bananas are **perfectly** fine. Don't throw them away.
      a. You shouldn't eat the bananas.    b. You can eat the bananas.

5. **YOUR TURN** Work with a partner. Do you think famous actors and athletes make too much money? Why or why not?

   *I think that professional athletes should be paid a lot because they work extremely hard. Nearly all of the athletes I like deserve the money they make.*

## Grammar: Tag questions

**6. Complete the chart.**

*Use tag questions to find out new information, to find out if someone agrees or disagrees with you, or to confirm something you believe is true. Tag questions are common in spoken English. If the statement is affirmative, the tag question is negative. If the statement is negative, the tag question is affirmative.*

| Simple present of *be* | Simple past of *be* |
|---|---|
| That's crazy, _____ it? <br> He**'s not** an actor, **is** he? | The acting **was** fabulous, **wasn't** it? <br> The acting **wasn't** good, _____ it? |

| Simple present | Simple past |
|---|---|
| That **seems** like too much, **doesn't** it? <br> That **doesn't seem** fair, _____ it? | She **admired** that actor, _____ she? <br> We **didn't see** that movie, **did** we? |

| Modals |
|---|
| Actors **shouldn't make** so much money, **should** they? <br> The actors _____ **get** a large portion of the money, **shouldn't** they? |

> Check your answers: Grammar reference, p. 110

**7. Circle the correct answers.**

1. He'll make a lot of money for that movie, **will** / **won't** he?
2. Carl didn't agree with you, **did** / **didn't** he?
3. Robert Downey Jr. is the highest paid actor in Hollywood, **is** / **isn't** he?
4. You haven't seen that movie yet, **have** / **haven't** you?
5. Actors shouldn't care what people think about them, **should** / **shouldn't** they?
6. You can go to the soccer game, **can** / **can't** you?
7. That wasn't a famous actor in the café, **was** / **wasn't** it?
8. Mary and Ron dislike reality TV shows, **do** / **don't** they?

**8. Complete the sentences with the correct tag questions.**

1. Sandra Bullock gives a lot of money to charity, _____doesn't she_____?
2. Basketball players make a lot of money doing TV commercials, _____?
3. You're buying the new Beyoncé album, _____?
4. Tom didn't make much money playing soccer last year, _____?
5. Larry shouldn't give up his dream of becoming famous, _____?
6. Jennifer Lawrence hasn't acted in a comedy, _____?
7. Angelina Jolie and Brad Pitt are married, _____?
8. You weren't at the last World Cup, _____?

## Speaking: It was great, right?

**9. YOUR TURN** Work with a partner. What does your partner think about these topics? Guess using tag questions.

- a popular movie
- a hip-hop musician
- a famous soccer player
- a reality TV star

> You liked the Avengers movies, didn't you?
>
> Yes, I did. The special effects were absolutely amazing, weren't they?
>
> Yeah. And the acting was great, right?

---

### Say it RIGHT!

Listen to the sentences. When you are sure about an answer, your voice goes down with the tag question. When you are unsure, your voice goes up.

*You liked the movie, **didn't you**?*
= You're pretty sure the person liked the movie, and you want confirmation.

*You liked the movie, **didn't you**?*
= You don't know if the person liked the movie, and you want to find out.

Use the correct intonation when you ask questions in Exercise 9, depending on how sure you are of your partner's answers.

### NOTICE IT

The tags *right* and *OK* can be used after statements with any verb tense.

*Let's stop talking and go to lunch, **OK**?*
*You haven't seen the Avengers movies, **right**?*

> Workbook, pp. 32–33

**REAL TALK** 5.2 HOW DO YOU PREPARE FOR A SPORTS EVENT?

# Lights, Camera, ACTION!

## Conversation: Getting ready for the game

**NOTICE IT**
| British English | American English |
|---|---|
| crisps | potato chips |
| match | game |
| take-away meal | take-out meal |

1. **REAL TALK** Watch or listen to the teenagers talk about how they prepare for a sports event. Check (✓) the things they mention.

   ☐ buying good shoes ☐ getting more sleep ☐ practicing
   ☐ drinking water ☐ listening to music ☐ stretching
   ☐ getting food ☐ listening to the coach ☐ swimming

2. **YOUR TURN** How do *you* prepare for a sports event? Tell your partner.

3. Listen to Elsa and Marcos talking about two soccer teams. Complete the conversation.

   **USEFUL LANGUAGE: Making a point**
   - as far as I'm concerned
   - it seems to me that
   - Not necessarily!
   - ✓ of course
   - That's a good point.
   - You're absolutely right.

   **Elsa:** I can't wait for the soccer championship on Saturday.
   **Marcos:** Me, neither. It's going to be a great game. ¹ *Of course*, Bayside is going to win.
   **Elsa:** ² _____ Clifton has an excellent head coach this year. I think they'll win.
   **Marcos:** No way! Bayside has won three years in a row, and they have the better team.
   **Elsa:** Well, they started pretty strong this year but ³ _____ they haven't been playing as well the last few weeks.
   **Marcos:** True, but that's because their star player was injured. He's better now, and he'll be playing on Saturday.
   **Elsa:** Oh, I didn't know that. But ⁴ _____, Clifton still has a chance. I mean, they won their last 10 games. And since they've never won the championship, they're going to really fight for it.
   **Marcos:** ⁵ _____ But they're going to have to fight extremely hard!
   **Elsa:** ⁶ _____ It's going to be exciting either way.

4. Practice the conversation with a partner.

5. **YOUR TURN** Work with a partner. Discuss one of the questions below or your own idea. Each person takes a different side, even if you don't really agree with it. Support your opinions with reasons.

| | Student A | Student B |
|---|---|---|
| Which singer is better? | Katy Perry | Demi Lovato |
| Which team is better? | Real Madrid | Santos |

# THE BOOK IS BETTER!
by Ethan Beck

Both the first Harry Potter book, *Harry Potter and the Sorcerer's Stone* and the first Harry Potter movie with the same name are extremely good. In my opinion, the book is slightly better.

There are many similarities between the book and the movie. The characters in the movie are as interesting as the book's characters. In addition, many parts of the plot are the same in the book and the movie, especially the first scene.

There are also some differences. First of all, Harry Potter has green eyes, but Daniel Radcliff, who played Harry Potter, has blue eyes. Secondly, many of the characters' parts in the movie are not nearly as big as they are in the book. For example, Nicholas Flamel, who created the stone, is barely seen in the movie. Mrs. Figg isn't in the movie at all!

Although both the book and the movie are good, I feel that the book is better because we learn more about the characters.

## Reading to write: A comparison/contrast essay

**6.** Look at the title of Ethan's essay and the photos. What do you think it's about? Read his essay to check.

### ● Focus on CONTENT
When you write a comparison/contrast essay, include this information:
- introduction: State your opinion.
- body: Give similarities and differences in two separate paragraphs.
- conclusion: Restate your opinion.

**7.** Read Ethan's essay again. What's his opinion? What similarities and differences does he give?

### ● Focus on LANGUAGE
Use *(not) as . . . as* to compare or contrast two things.
The book is **as good as** the movie.
The movie is **not as long as** the book.
You can also use adverbs with *(not) as . . . as*.
The characters are **just as interesting as** the plot.
That movie star is **nowhere near as rich as** his wife.
The first scene is **not nearly as exciting as** the last.
The second book is **not quite as good as** the first.

**8.** Find the phrases in Ethan's essay with *(not) as . . . as*.

**9.** Complete the sentences with the correct form of *(not) as . . . as*.

1. The movie *Alice in Wonderland* is <u>just as strange as</u> the book. (just / strange)
2. In the book, the Cat in the Hat is _____ he is in the movie. (not nearly / tall)
3. The movie *Charlotte's Web* is _____ the book. (magical)
4. The movie is _____ the book. (not quite / good)
5. In the movie *The Jungle Book*, the Croc is _____ he is in the book. (nowhere near / scary)
6. The book *Polar Express* is _____ the movie. (not colorful)

## ✏️ Writing: Your comparison/contrast essay

### ○ PLAN
Choose a book that has been made into a movie to write about. Complete the diagram.

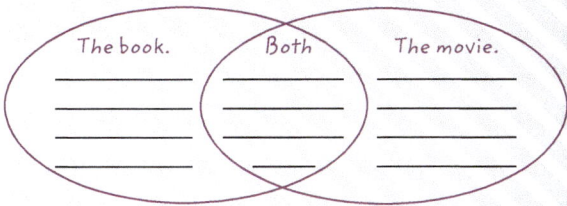

*The book.* — *Both* — *The movie.*

### ○ WRITE
Write a comparison/contrast essay. Use your notes to help you. Use *(not) as . . . as* and adverb + *(not) as . . . as*. Write at least 150 words.

### ○ CHECK
Check your writing. Can you answer "yes" to these questions?

- Is information from the Focus on Content box in your essay?
- Do you use *(not) as . . . as* and adverb + *(not) as . . . as* correctly?

# Getting Paid for Your OPINIONS

It seems that everyone is a critic these days. People are saying what they think about movies, TV shows, books, fashion, and celebrities on social networking pages and blog posts. But what does it take to become a critic that people listen to and respect?

First of all, to be a good critic, you need to be a good writer. Your ideas need to be clear and organized. You also have to develop your own style. Is your writing smart and serious? Or is it humorous and quirky? People have to want to read your opinions and care about what you say! Secondly, you need to have a lot of experience in your field. Critics often make comparisons in their reviews. So, if you're a movie critic, you need to know about a lot of different movies – past and present. You should also know about actors, directors, and even cinematography (how the movie is filmed). If you're a book critic, you need to have read a lot of books and be familiar with many authors. Thirdly, decide what media you want to use. Do you want to write for a magazine or a website? Do you want to make video reviews or work on a TV show?

It can be extremely difficult to make a career as a critic, but these people did it.

**TARAN ADARSH** is a movie critic in India. He started working for a weekly movie magazine at 15. Today, he reviews Bollywood movies online and hosts a TV show, which includes movie reviews and interviews with Bollywood stars.

**JACKSON MURPHY**, who goes by the name Lights Camera Jackson, is a teenage movie critic in the United States. He writes online movie reviews that are extremely popular.

**KELLY OSBOURNE**, who is British, is a famous fashion critic. She was on a TV show called *Fashion Police*. She says what she likes and dislikes about clothes that celebrities wear.

If they do it, you can, too, right?

## Culture: An article about becoming a critic

1. Look at the title. What ways do you know that people can get paid for their opinions?
2. Read and listen to the article. What three things does the article say you need to do to be a critic?
3. Read the article again. Match the beginnings of the sentences with the correct endings.

   1. You need to have an interesting writing style ____
   2. Movie critics need to know ____
   3. Critics not only write, ____
   4. Taran Adarsh is ____
   5. Jackson Murphy is ____
   6. Kelly Osbourne is ____

   a. a movie critic and TV host.
   b. a fashion critic.
   c. about actors and directors.
   d. so that people want to read your opinions.
   e. a young movie critic.
   f. but they also give their opinions on Web videos and TV.

4. **YOUR TURN** Work with a partner. Imagine you are a movie, book, or fashion critic on a TV show. Give your opinion about a recent movie, book, or fashion trend.

## DID YOU KNOW...?

Most critics try not to include "spoilers" in their reviews. A spoiler is when you tell someone information about a movie that gives away a surprise.

**BE CURIOUS** Find out about trends and trendsetters. What do Saeko and Yuko do? (Workbook, p. 81)

5.3 TRENDSETTERS

# UNIT 5 REVIEW

## Vocabulary

**1. Circle the correct answers.**

1. We **appreciate** / **think** movie stars who help other people.
2. I **feel** / **respect** that you care too much about following trends.
3. Mike **dislikes** / **prefers** reading to watching movies.
4. I really **admire** / **recommend** my sister for becoming her soccer team's captain.
5. Lori **hates** / **appreciates** reality TV, and she gets mad at me when I watch it.
6. Kayla **feels** / **recommends** Ursula K. Le Guin's books.
7. My mother **hates** / **thinks** that I should watch less TV.
8. I **respect** / **prefer** my science teacher for all of his hard work.

## Grammar

**2. Put the words in order to make sentences.**

1. who / I / slightly strange / comedians / prefer / are

   _____

2. to schools / she / that / gives / nearly all her money / need help

   _____

3. started a trend / the athlete, / who / won a gold medal, / in sports clothing

   _____

4. were fairly expensive, / we / which / last week / bought concert tickets,

   _____

5. whose / moved / to Hollywood / house we bought / the actor

   _____

6. in the city, / our favorite singer / where / we met / we went / to a concert

   _____

**3. Match the beginnings of the sentences with the correct tag questions.**

1. Nancy was perfectly calm before the concert, ____
2. Julie works extremely hard, ____
3. Vanessa isn't in that movie, ____
4. Jin-Hee hasn't donated to our cause, ____
5. Paulina will make a new album, ____
6. Kate didn't win the race, ____

a. is she?
b. did she?
c. won't she?
d. wasn't she?
e. has she?
f. doesn't she?

## Useful language

**4. Circle the correct answers.**

**Lynn:** I really dislike reality TV shows. [1]**It seems to me that / That's a good point** the people who are on them are famous for doing nothing!

**Jeff:** [2]**Of course / Not necessarily!** For example, on *Project Runway*, the reality stars are pretty good fashion designers.

**Lynn:** Well, [3]**as far as I'm concerned / that's a good point**. But I don't mean shows like that. I mean ones where it's just about people's everyday lives. [4]**As far as I'm concerned / You're absolutely right**, they're just a waste of time.

**Jeff:** [5]**It seems to me that / You're absolutely right!** I hate those kinds of reality shows, too. [6]**Not necessarily / Of course**, a lot of people disagree. They're extremely popular.

**Lynn:** I know! Nearly all of my friends like them.

---

**PROGRESS CHECK: Now I can . . .**

☐ express opinions about different topics.
☐ give reasons why I'd support a cause.
☐ ask questions to confirm and find out information.
☐ make a point.
☐ write a comparison/contrast essay.
☐ give my opinion about a movie, book, or fashion trend.

## Uncover Your Knowledge
# UNITS 1–5 Review Game

**TEAM 1 START**

- In 30 seconds, tell a teammate about how your interests in movies or music have changed from five years ago. Use expressions like *(not) crazy about* or *really into/can't stand*.

- Use each of these phrasal verbs in a sentence: *sign up, give up, get along, turn into*.

- Tell a teammate about something that happened last weekend. Use the verbs *watch* and *hear*. Then say what you were doing while those things happened.

- In 60 seconds, explain the difference between a reporter and a blogger, and in what media you'll find an article, a news report, and an interview.

- Role-play a difficult situation with a teammate. Show concern that your teammate's best friend is moving away. Your teammate responds.

- Name the top three priorities you have in life, and explain why they are important to you.

- Say 3–5 rules to have a good party. Talk about things that are possible and things that are always true.

- In 30 seconds, describe someone in class using three adjectives of personal qualities. Your teammates must guess who it is.

- Play "cause and effect." Tell a teammate a cause, such as *One day, I'll have earned a million dollars...* Your teammate responds with a phrase such as *since* or *because of* to introduce the effect: *since I learned to speak English well*. See how many you can say in 2 minutes.

- Describe two things that you didn't use to do 10 years ago that you do now. Then describe two things that you often did 10 years ago that you don't do now.

- Talk about your plans for the future. Use the verbs *predict, graduate, plan,* and *become*.

## INSTRUCTIONS:

- Make teams and choose game pieces.
- Put your game pieces on your team's START.
- Flip a coin to see who goes first.
- Read the first challenge. Can you do it correctly?

    Yes ➔ Continue to the next challenge.

    No ➔ Lose your turn.

The first team to do all of the challenges wins!

- GRAMMAR
- VOCABULARY
- USEFUL LANGUAGE

## TEAM 2
### START

- Use *be going to* and *will* to make predictions and talk about another classmate's plans for the next five years.
- In 15 seconds, name seven different ways to cook food.
- Role-play with a teammate. Your teammate is a famous athlete or celebrity. You are a reporter. Ask questions about where and how long they've been playing or performing. The teammate answers.
- Tell a partner how to cook your favorite dish. Use cooking instructions, the steps in the process, and amounts.
- Describe how your English was before you took this class. How long had you been studying before and how had your English been?
- Predict achievements for two of your classmates. Use at least two of these nouns: *an award, a record, volunteer work, a business, a project*.
- With a teammate, ask and answer three questions to find out information or if someone agrees/disagrees, or if something is/isn't true. Use tag questions.
- Describe two foods you like and two that you don't like. Use adjectives such as *crunchy* or *sour* to describe them.
- Make predictions about what a famous celebrity and/or athlete will have achieved in the next five years.
- Say five sentences about what you did last night. Use these adverbs of degree: *hardly, nearly, pretty, extremely, perfectly*.
- Share an opinion with your teammate. Your teammate should disagree politely and explain why. Continue the conversation for 30 seconds, remembering to use phrases to make a point.
- Ask a teammate four questions about what he/she would/wouldn't eat in imaginary situations. Use *would (not)* in your questions. Your teammate answers.
- Use different verbs to express opinions about movies, music, and sports. Say one positive and one negative sentence about each topic.
- Use relative clauses (*who, where,* or *whose*) to talk about your favorite and least favorite athletes and celebrities.

Units 1–5 Review | 53

## Past tense review, p. 5

### Simple past

*Use simple past statements to talk about past events and activities.*

| Regular | Irregular |
|---|---|
| What **did** you **believe**? | What **did** she **write**? |
| I **believed** everything on the Internet. | She **wrote** a report for school. |
| We **didn't believe** the story. | She **didn't write** a blog post. |

### Past continuous

*Use the past continuous to talk about activities that were in progress in the past. To form the past continuous use* was/were + present participle (-ing form).

What **were** you **doing** wrong?
I **was using** incorrect information. I **wasn't checking** my facts.
Where **was** he **going**? He **was going** to class.
What **were** they **watching**? They **were watching** the news.

### Present perfect

*Use the present perfect to talk about experiences that happened at an indefinite time in the past. To form the present perfect, use* has/have + the past participle.

Who **has used** Snopes.com?
Many people **have used** the website! I **haven't used** it before.
He **has used** it. He **hasn't used** it.

**1. Correct the sentences.**

1. Simple past: We eat dinner while we watching TV.

2. Past continuous: They were listen to a Web interview.

3. Present perfect: What has you did in class this year?

## Review of *used to* + infinitive and *would*, p. 7

*Use* used to *or* would *for things that happened repeatedly in the past but don't happen now.*

| | |
|---|---|
| Where **did** she **use to do** research?<br>   She **used to do** it at the library.<br>   She **didn't use to have** a computer. | **Did** you **use to go** to the library?<br>   Yes, I **did**.<br>   No, I **didn't**. |
| When **would** you **watch** the news?<br>   I **would watch** it at 6:00.<br>   I **wouldn't watch** it online. | **Would** they **watch** the news every night?<br>   Yes, they **would**.<br>   No, I/you/he/she/they/we **wouldn't**. |

*Use* used to, *not* would, *for situations that happened in the past.*

I **used to live** in Los Angeles. (NOT: ~~I would live~~ in Los Angeles.)

**2. Circle the correct answers. Sometimes both answers are possible.**

1. After school, I **used to** / **would** go to my friend's house to play.

2. Franco **didn't use to** / **wouldn't** live in New York when he was young.

3. Katie and Paulina **used to** / **would** text each other every day.

4. You **didn't use to** / **wouldn't** have long hair.

5. We **used to** / **would** ride our bikes every day.

# Present perfect with present perfect continuous, p. 15

### Present perfect continuous

*Use the present perfect continuous for experiences that happened at an indefinite time in the past and continue to the present.*

| | |
|---|---|
| Where **have** you **been climbing**? <br> I **have been climbing** at home. <br> I **haven't been climbing** in the mountains. | **Have** you **been training** a lot? <br> Yes, I **have**. <br> No, I **haven't**. |
| What **has** she **been doing**? <br> She **has been running** a club. <br> She **hasn't been working** in an office. | **Has** she **been climbing** for a long time? <br> Yes, she **has**. <br> No, she **hasn't**. |

### Present perfect vs. present perfect continuous

*Remember to use the present perfect for experiences that happened at an indefinite time in the past and are now complete. Use the present perfect to emphasize the result.*

He used to be a professional rock climber, but he **has stopped** climbing.

*Use the present perfect continuous to emphasize the action.*

She **has been climbing** since she was four.

**1. Rewrite the sentences in the present perfect continuous when possible. When not possible, write X.**

1. Where have you taken a Portuguese class?
   _____

2. Mia hasn't gone to school this week.
   _____

3. I haven't signed up for classes yet.
   _____

4. Doug has kept up with his homework.
   _____

5. My cousin has been determined to win that race.
   _____

# Past perfect and past perfect continuous, p. 17

### Past perfect continuous

*Use the past perfect continuous for experiences that started in the past and continued up until another time in the past.*

| | |
|---|---|
| What **had** they **been doing**? <br> They **had been using** cell phones before the program started. <br> They **hadn't been using** email. | **Had** they **been using** cell phones? <br> Yes, they **had**. <br> No, they **hadn't**. |

### Past perfect vs. past perfect continuous

*Remember to use the past perfect to refer to something that happened before a specific time in the past. Use the past perfect to emphasize the result.*

Fifty people **had signed** up this year.   I **hadn't heard** of that job.

*Use the past perfect continuous to emphasize the action.*

I **had been working** with Helen for 6 months.

**2. Circle the correct answers. Sometimes both answers are possible.**

1. I **hadn't gotten / hadn't been getting** along with my brother all summer.
2. Farah **had been / had been being** motivated to learn to swim.
3. Had you **written / been writing** a blog?
4. Jack had already **gone / been going** to the store when I got home.

## Future review, p. 25

| will | be going to |
|---|---|
| Use will for predictions. | Use going to for planned actions and events. |
| What classes **will** David **take**?<br>He **will take** Russian classes.<br>He **won't take** French. | Where **is** he **going to** live?<br>He **is going to live in** to Houston.<br>He **isn't going to live** in his hometown. |
| | When **are** you **going to work**?<br>I'm **going to work** on Sunday.<br>I'm **not going to work** on Saturday. |
| **Present continuous** | **Simple present** |
| Use the present continuous for planned actions and events. | Use the simple present for scheduled future events. |
| What classes **is** he **taking** next year?<br>He **is taking** advanced science.<br>He **isn't taking** art classes. | Where **does** he **plan** to go?<br>He **plans** to go to the ISS.<br>He **doesn't plan** to go to Russia. |
| Where **are** they **driving** tomorrow?<br>They **are driving** to Florida.<br>They **aren't driving** to California. | When **do** you **have** your next yoga class?<br>I **have** a class tomorrow.<br>I **don't have** a class on Friday. |

**1. Correct the future forms in the sentences. Correct one word in each sentence.**

1. Jack hates flying, so he will fly in space one day.
2. When are you go to start a business?
3. What time does the bus left tomorrow morning?
4. Cindy is take a lot of science classes this year.

## Future continuous and future perfect, p. 27

| Future continuous | |
|---|---|
| Use the future continuous to describe something that will be in progress in the future. To form the future continuous, use will + be + the -ing form of a verb. | |
| Who **will** be **volunteering**?<br>We **will be volunteering**.<br>They **won't be volunteering**. | **Will** you be **volunteering**?<br>Yes, I **will**.<br>No, I **won't**. |
| **Future perfect** | |
| Use the future perfect to describe something that is going to be finished at a certain time in the future. To form the future perfect, use will + have + past participle. | |
| How much trash **will** she **have collected** in 20 years?<br>She **will have collected** a lot of trash.<br>She **won't have earned** much money. | **Will** she **have collected** a lot of trash?<br>Yes, she **will have**.<br>No, she **won't have**. |

**2. Write answers for the questions.**

1. Where will Susan be studying next year? (Brazil)
   _____

2. Will you have graduated from high school before your 18th birthday? (no)
   _____

3. How much money will you have saved by the time you start college? ($3,000)
   _____

4. Will you be going to summer camp this year? (yes)
   _____

# First conditional review; zero conditional, p. 35

*Use the first conditional to show results or possible results of future actions.*
*Use* if, when, *or* unless *and the simple present in the main clause. Use* will (not) *and the base form of a verb in the result clause.*

**If** your skin **smells** like garlic, a mosquito probably **won't bite** you!
You**'ll have to go** to a restaurant with a fugu-trained chef, **unless** you **want** it to be your last meal!

*Use the zero conditional to show a result of an action that is always true.*
*Use* if, when, *or* unless *and the simple present in the main clause and the simple present in the result clause.*

A poisonous gas **comes** out of an onion **when** you **cut** or **fry** it.
**If** the gas **gets** into your eyes, your body **makes** tears to wash it out.

1. **Correct the sentences. Correct one word in each sentence.**
    1. When I will go to my favorite restaurant, I usually order the same dish.
    2. We'll have to have the party inside if it will rain tomorrow.
    3. If Jenna makes spicy food again, I don't eat it.
    4. I make lemonade unless the store is out of lemons. I hope they have them.
    5. When I go to a dinner party, I always will bring a dessert.

# Second conditional review, p. 37

*Use the second conditional to describe imaginary situations and possible consequences. Use* if *or* unless *+ simple past for the imaginary situation. Use* would (not) *+ base form of the verb for the possible consequence.*

### Yes/No questions

**Would** you **eat** it again **if** you **had** the chance?
Yes, I **would**. / No, I **wouldn't**.
**If** I **saw** it on a menu, I **would eat** it again.
I **wouldn't eat** it again **if** you **paid** me.

### Wh- questions

**If** I **wanted** to eat *chapulines* again, where **would** I **get** them?
You probably **wouldn't find** them **unless** you **went** to Mexico.

*For* be, *use* was *or* were *after I.*

I'd try *chapulines* if I **was** in Mexico.
If I **were** in Mexico, I'd try *chapulines*.

2. **Complete the sentences with the correct forms of the verbs.**
    1. _____ you _____ (try) the local food if you _____ (be) in another country?
    2. I _____ (make) a Moroccan stew if I _____ (have) a tagine.
    3. If Carl and Joe _____ (not have) a car, they _____ (walk) to the store.
    4. What _____ Lori _____ (cook) if her parents _____ (come) to dinner?
    5. We _____ (not eat) fast food unless we _____ (be) in a hurry.

# Defining and non-defining relative clauses, p. 45

*Use defining relative clauses with* who, which, that, where, *and* whose *to give necessary information about a noun. The sentence has a different meaning without the clause.*

People **who make clothing** should be treated fairly.
Celebrities **that give money to organizations** often help bring attention to important causes.
Some of the money went to help people **whose homes had been ruined**.

*Use non-defining relative clauses with* who, which, where, *and* whose *to give additional information about a noun. The clause can be left out of the sentence and it still makes sense.*

Bono, **who is the lead singer of U2**, is admired for his charity work.
The Angel Network, **which Oprah started in 1998**, has raised more than $50,000,000.
They saw the effects of global warming in Sochi, **where the Olympics took place**.

**1. Complete the sentences with** who, which, where, **or** whose.

1. My uncle, _____ was on a sitcom in the 1990s, hosts a talk show.
2. The athletes gave money to schools _____ soccer teams didn't have uniforms.
3. The Always Dream Foundation, _____ was started by Olympic skater Kristi Yamaguchi, gives computers to an after-school program.
4. Brazil, _____ the 2014 World Cup was held, will host the 2016 Summer Olympics.

# Tag questions, p. 47

*Use tag questions to find out new information, to find out if someone agrees or disagrees with you, or to confirm something you believe is true. Tag questions are common in spoken English. If the statement is affirmative, the tag question is negative. If the statement is negative, the tag question is affirmative.*

| Simple present of *be* | Simple past of *be* |
| --- | --- |
| That**'s** crazy, **isn't** it? <br> He**'s not** an actor, **is** he? | The acting **was** fabulous, **wasn't** it? <br> The acting **wasn't** good, **was** it? |
| **Simple present** | **Simple past** |
| That **seems** like too much, **doesn't** it? <br> That **doesn't seem** fair, **does** it? | She **admired** that actor, **didn't** she? <br> We **didn't see** that movie, **did** we? |
| **Modals** | |
| Actors **shouldn't make** so much money, **should** they? <br> The actors **should get** a large portion of the money, **shouldn't** they? | |
| **Other forms** | |
| Future with *will* | We**'ll go** see that new movie, **won't** we? |
| Present perfect | You **haven't been** on TV before, **have** you? |

**2. Complete the tag questions.**

1. Lisa got Willow Smith's autograph, _____ ?
2. You haven't read *The Hunger Games*, _____ ?
3. Your cousins aren't fans of Real Madrid, _____ ?
4. We should get tickets for the 9:00 show, _____ ?

This page intentionally left blank.

# The Smart HOUSE

**CLIL PROJECT**

1. Here are some jobs that can now be done by a computer instead of a person. Label the pictures with the correct words.

   babysitter    butler    personal assistant    secretary

   **1** _____  **2** _____  **3** _____  **4** _____

**Discovery EDUCATION**
**2.4 THE HOUSE OF THE FUTURE**

2. Watch the video. Check (✓) the activities Cleopatra can do.

   1. Raise the blinds _____
   2. Paint the room _____
   3. Change the music _____
   4. Discuss the weather _____
   5. Manage the shopping _____
   6. Do the ironing _____
   7. Cook dinner _____
   8. Open the front door _____

3. Complete the sentences with the correct words.

   1. Will it even change the music based on your _____?
   2. She mostly lives on a box that we have down in our _____ room.
   3. Cleopatra uses radio _____ ID technology.
   4. It will automatically reorder anything that you _____.
   5. That's a lot of money, but if we're going to live in _____ like these in the future . . .

**PROJECT**

Imagine your own "house of the future." Is it in the city or the country? Is it in the sky or underwater? Does your house use the latest technology? Look at the model poster, then make your own.

Write a description of your house here. What does it look like?

What technology does your house have? What does it do?

Draw a floor plan of your house.

# What's in OUR FOOD?

1. **Label the pictures with the correct words.**

   | fats and proteins | natural sugar | processed food | salt |

   1. _____  2. _____  3. _____  4. _____

2. **Watch the video. Complete the sentences with the correct words.**

   | natural sugar | preservatives |
   | nutritional information | processed food |

   1. But now more than ever, factories are creating _____.
   2. . . . it often has salt, sugar, _____, coloring, and flavoring all added . . .
   3. When you're shopping, it's important to check for _____.
   4. The _____ in fruit is much healthier than processed sugar.

   **4.4 YOU ARE WHAT YOU EAT**

3. **Number the items 1–5 in the order you see them.**

   ____ a man juggling
   ____ cows eating grass
   ____ two children writing
   ____ a giant cow
   ____ cheese

**PROJECT** You are trying to eat healthier foods. Make a food journal for the items you ate yesterday. Decide if the foods you ate were *low*, *medium*, or *high* in the areas on the chart below.

| Meal | Item | Fats and proteins | Natural sugars | Salt | Processed Food |
|---|---|---|---|---|---|
| Breakfast | toast with butter | high in fat, low in protein | low | medium | no |
|  | orange juice | low | high | low | no |
|  | yogurt | high in protein | medium | low | no |
| Lunch |  |  |  |  |  |
| Dinner |  |  |  |  |  |

Study your chart. Are you eating too much of one type of food and not enough of another? Write down your ideas.

This page intentionally left blank.

# Uncover 4 Combo A
Lynne Robertson

## Workbook

CAMBRIDGE UNIVERSITY PRESS

Discovery EDUCATION

# 1 Tell Me About It!

## VOCABULARY  Media

**1 Label the pictures with the correct words. One word is used more than once.**

| article | interview | the news | reporter |
| blogger | headline | paper | review |

1. _____
2. _____
3. _____
4. _____
5. _____
6. _____
7. _____
8. _____
9. _____

**2 Circle the correct answers.**

Gina: Have you seen the ¹**article / news** yet?

Felix: No, what happened?

Gina: That ²**interview / reporter** you like quit. There's a new person reporting the news now.

Felix: Oh, well. I have to watch a ³**paper / report** every night because we talk about current events in my civics class.

Gina: Do you have to watch TV news? There's a ⁴**blogger / paper** I really like. He writes about interesting issues on his website.

Felix: Well, we're supposed to discuss local news in class. I can just read the local ⁵**paper / review**.

Gina: It's online, too, you know. Here, look. The ⁶**interview / headline** says that some roads will be closed this weekend. And there's an ⁷**interview / review** with the local police explaining what alternate routes to take.

Felix: That's kind of dull. The paper has this ⁸**blogger / article** about an old building the city wants to tear down, but some people want to preserve it. The mayor is holding a town hall meeting to discuss the issue on Friday.

Gina: That's a good issue to talk about in your class. Oh, look! There's a ⁹**review / headline** of the latest *Star Wars* movie. It opens this Friday. We should go!

Felix: Sure, we can go after the town hall meeting.

**3 Answer the questions. Use your own information.**

1. Where do you get the news?
   *I get the news from the radio and online.*
   _____

2. Where do your parents or grandparents get the news?
   _____

3. What kind of news articles do you like to read?
   _____

4. What kind of reviews interest you?
   _____

5. What is an interesting interview you have seen or heard?
   _____

## GRAMMAR Past tense review: Simple past, past continuous, and present perfect

**1** Complete the chart.

---

**Simple past**

What _did_ you _watch_?

I _____ (watch) a news report online.

I _____ (not watch) it on television.

What _____ the reporter _____ (say)?

He _____ (say) the storm caused the power to go out.

But he _____ (not say) how long it would be out.

**Past continuous**

What _____ you _____ (do) when the power went out?

I **was driving** my car. I _____ (not use) my cell phone. That's dangerous.

**Present perfect**

Who **has seen** that new reality series?

I _____ (not see) it yet. But Laura _____ (see) every episode. She loves it.

---

**2** Write each sentence in the simple past and in the past continuous.

1. Juan works at the store on weekends.

   _Juan worked at the store on weekends._

   _Juan was working at the store on weekends._

2. Jenny rides a bike in the morning.

   Jenny _____.

   Jenny _____.

3. Tom and Gina study Chinese.

   _____

   _____

4. We don't play football in the park.

   _____

   _____

**3** Look at Exercise 2. Complete the questions and answers with the present perfect forms of the verbs.

1. A: Who _has learned_ (learn) how to read Chinese?

   B: _Tom and Gina have learned how to read Chinese._

2. A: Who _____ (work) on weekends before?

   B: _____

3. A: Who _____ (ride) a bike in the morning?

   B: _____

4. A: Who _____ (not play) football in the park?

   B: _____

## Past passive and present perfect passive

**4** Complete the chart.

---

**Past passive**

The article _was posted_ (post) online.

The photographs _____ (post) last week. But they _____ (not post) by me.

**Present perfect passive**

The video _has been watched_ (watch) by over 3 million people!

It _____ (see) in over 30 countries. But it _____ (not see) in the artist's own country.

---

**5** Rewrite the sentences. Use the forms in parentheses.

1. Someone used a fact-checking site to prove that the legend was false. (past passive)

   _A fact-checking site was used to prove that the legend was false._

2. No one posted the game scores to the school website. (present perfect passive)

   _____

3. Over 60,000 people attended the summer music festival. (past passive)

   _____

4. A cell phone didn't record the event. (present perfect passive)

   _____

## VOCABULARY  Time expressions

**1  Read the sentences. Then circle the action that started or happened first.**

1. My dad was living in a small town **before** he met my mother.
   a. ~~My dad lived in a small town.~~ *(circled)*
   b. He met my mother.

2. **After** they got married, they moved to the city.
   a. They got married.
   b. They moved to the city.

3. My dad was working as a reporter **while** my mom was finishing college.
   a. He worked as a reporter.
   b. She finished college.

4. She got a job as a computer programmer **as soon as** she finished college.
   a. She got a job as a computer programmer.
   b. She finished college.

5. I was born **by the time** my mom was 30.
   a. I was born.
   b. My mom was 30.

6. She's been working part-time **since** I was born.
   a. She worked part-time.
   b. I was born.

7. **Whenever** I had a question about my computer homework, she helped me.
   a. I had a question about my computer homework.
   b. She helped me.

8. **Every time** there's been a new smartphone, she's been the first to try it.
   a. There's a new smartphone.
   b. She was the first to try it.

**2  Complete the sentences with the correct words.**

1. *As soon as* I wake up in the morning, I take a shower. (As soon as / By the time)

2. _____ he eats breakfast, my dad checks his email. (Until / While)

3. He rode his bike to school _____ he learned to drive. (every time / until)

4. She's been playing video games _____ she was six. (since / whenever)

5. _____ I go to school in the morning, I charge my phone battery. (Before / Since)

6. _____ I got the text, I had already left. (By the time / Every time)

7. _____ I use the school computer, I forget to sign out. (As / Every time)

8. Hannah texted me _____ the game had finished. (after / whenever)

9. _____ I was researching my paper online, I saw the headlines on a news website. (As / Until)

10. _____ my smartphone rings in class, my teacher gets angry. (Before / Whenever)

11. There was nobody in the library _____ I left last night. (when / as soon as)

**3  Use the time expressions from Exercise 1 to combine sentences. More than one answer may be possible.**

1. My laptop broke. I was watching my friend's video clips.
   *My laptop broke while I was watching my friend's video clips.*

2. The game had ended. I texted my dad.
   _____

3. I bought tickets for the concert. They went on sale at noon.
   _____

4. The band was playing their last song. I recorded it with my smartphone.
   _____

5. I studied for the test. I was taking the bus to school.
   _____

# GRAMMAR  Review of *used to* + infinitive and *would*

**1** Read the sentences and check (✓) the correct columns.

|   | Thing that happened repeatedly in the past but doesn't happen now | Situation that happened in the past |
|---|---|---|
| 1. I used to live on a houseboat when I was a baby. | | ✓ |
| 2. My brother used to study German. | | |
| 3. Jack would always win when we played tennis. | | |
| 4. I would watch the news at night. | | |
| 5. My family didn't use to own a television. | | |
| 6. I didn't use to like to eat vegetables. | | |

**2** Complete the conversation. Use *used to*, *would*, or the simple past. More than one answer may be possible.

Marissa: Hey, Gan. Where in Thailand ¹ *did you use to* live when you were young?

Gan: Well, when I was very young, I ² _____ in Bangkok. We lived on a *khlong*, or canal.

Marissa: Interesting. Did you ³ _____ swimming a lot?

Gan: No! We never ⁴ _____ go in the water.

Marissa: ⁵ _____ you go fishing?

Gan: No, we ⁶ _____. But my family ⁷ _____ go to the floating market.

Marissa: What ⁸ _____ you buy at the market?

Gan: We ⁹ _____ buy fruit and vegetables. And we ¹⁰ _____ eat dinner from kitchens on the boats and drink coconut drinks.

Marissa: How often ¹¹ _____ eat at the market?

Gan: We ¹² _____ eat there a couple times a week. It was fun.

**3** Correct the sentences. Use *used to*, *would*, or the simple past. More than one answer may be possible.

*played*
1. Kevin ~~would play~~ in the snow last vacation.
2. We would live in Hawaii when I was younger.
3. My grandparents didn't used to use their new computer until I showed them how.
4. I used to play my video game at 8:00 last night.
5. My family was buying vegetables at the store until we started our garden.

**4** Answer the questions using *used to* or *would*. Use your own information.

1. Where did you live when you were young?
   _____
   _____

2. What music did you listen to when you were young?
   _____
   _____

3. What games did you play with your friends?
   _____
   _____

4. What movies or TV shows did you watch?
   _____
   _____

## CONVERSATION — Expressing interest and disinterest

**1 Put the words in the correct order to make sentences.**

1. right / really / the / I'm / playing / into / guitar / now / .

   *I'm really into playing the guitar right now.*

2. crazy / live / I'm / not / about / music / .

   _____

3. I'm / that / into / not / music videos / watching / .

   _____

4. all / bands / I'm / about / punk / .

   _____

5. stand / music / I / can't / pop / .

   _____

6. about / I'm / new / this / video / crazy / .

   _____

**2 Complete the conversation with the correct phrases. More than one answer may be possible.**

| ✓all about | crazy about | not that into |
|---|---|---|
| can't stand | not crazy about | really into |

**Paul:** Have you watched my new music video yet?

**Ellie:** No, I haven't. Sorry. I'm ¹ *all about* this new John Mayer video right now.

**Paul:** Ugh! I ² _____ him!

**Ellie:** Really? But he plays guitar, like you.

**Paul:** Yeah, but we play different kinds of music. I like alternative and punk. I'm ³ _____ his singer-songwriter sound.

**Ellie:** Oh, well. How about Ellie Goulding? I'm ⁴ _____ her this year. She's amazing!

**Paul:** Her music and voice are OK, but I'm ⁵ _____ her like you are. She's still too pop for me.

**Ellie:** Oh, are you still ⁶ _____ Green Day?

**Paul:** Of course! They're my favorite!

## READING TO WRITE

**1** Number the parts of an informational blog post in order from 1–4.

_____ Give details about what you did or saw.

_____ Give information about the event in the future or similar events.

_____ Give general information about the event.

_____ Give your opinion about the event.

**2** Use Exercise 1 to number the parts of this informational blog post in order from 1–4.

### BATTLE OF THE BANDS | Lake High School

by Hailey Morgan

_____ Battle of the Bands takes place twice during the school year. The next one takes place in early January. Finalists go to the state finals in April.

_____ I went to Battle of the Bands at our high school last Saturday. It's an event for local high school bands to compete to win. The audience votes by cheering loudly for their favorite band. So it's up to the audience themselves to make some noise for the winner.

_____ I thought the band that won, The Closers, was really good. But I'm not that into rock and roll. I was crazy about the all-girl rap band, Tiger Lily. They were awesome. I myself would like to try rapping!

_____ Before the bands played, the school band played a song. Then the bands came out. Each band got to play three songs. After a band was done, the drama club performed a dance or comedy act while the next band set up. They really challenged themselves with some crazy dancing this year! The whole event took about three hours.

**3** Find the examples of reflexive and emphatic pronouns in Hailey's blog. Underline the reflexive pronouns. Circle the emphatic ones.

**4** Read the blog post in Exercise 2 again. Answer the questions.

1. What was the event?
   _The event was Battle of the Bands._

2. When was it?
   _____

3. Where was it?
   _____

4. Who competes?
   _____

5. How do they win?
   _____

6. Who won the contest?
   _____

7. Which band did Hailey like?
   _____

# 2 Best Foot Forward

**VOCABULARY** Personal qualities

**1** Find nine more words for personal qualities.

| B | L | H | Q | S | T | R | I | C | T | T | J |
|---|---|---|---|---|---|---|---|---|---|---|---|
| I | E | A | S | Y | G | O | I | N | G | R | W |
| P | X | R | L | F | S | F | T | I | D | C | A |
| A | R | D | O | G | C | V | Z | S | E | Q | B |
| S | J | W | M | O | T | I | V | A | T | E | D |
| S | S | O | I | M | P | A | T | I | E | N | T |
| I | H | R | U | G | F | H | F | N | R | J | V |
| O | Y | K | O | O | Z | C | S | H | M | U | C |
| N | V | I | D | R | R | L | T | C | I | N | A |
| A | J | N | B | P | Z | A | G | S | N | G | R |
| T | S | G | T | A | L | E | N | T | E | D | B |
| E | S | O | C | I | A | B | L | E | D | I | D |

**2** Complete the conversation with the correct words from Activity 1. More than one answer may be possible.

**Tim:** I think Kyla can win the singing competition. She's very ¹ _passionate_ and you can hear it in her voice. And she's ² _____, too. It just seems easy for her to sing beautifully. She doesn't have to try as hard as everyone else.

**Amy:** Yes, but John has a chance to win the competition, too. It's not as easy for him, but he is very ³ _____ to improve. And he spends all of his time practicing the same song over and over. He is very ⁴ _____.

**Tim:** Yeah, well, John can't make any mistakes because his coach is so ⁵ _____. On top of that, the coach is ⁶ _____, so John has to learn quickly.

**Amy:** Well, you know who needs a tougher coach? Noah! He doesn't try hard enough. He is too ⁷ _____. It's lucky he's ⁸ _____ and chats with the judges. They like him for that.

**Tim:** What about Callie? She's the opposite of Noah. She's so ⁹ _____ that she never chats with the judges.

**Amy:** You're right. And she's so afraid of making mistakes, it seems like she almost doesn't care about winning. The judges don't like it when you don't show that you're ¹⁰ _____. I think she'll go home next.

**3** Answer the questions with the words from Exercise 1 and your own information.

1. Describe someone you know who is easy-going.
   _My friend Alicia is easy-going. She doesn't get upset about anything. She acts the same if she gets a good or bad grade on a test._

2. Do you know someone who is talented? What is he or she good at?
   _____

3. Do you know someone who is hard-working? What makes him or her hard-working?
   _____

4. Name two personal qualities that you have. Describe them.
   _____
   _____

5. Describe two personal qualities you wish you had. How would these qualities help you?
   _____
   _____

8 | Unit 2

## GRAMMAR  Present perfect with present perfect continuous

**1** Put the words in the correct order to make sentences.

1. surfing / He / time / been / long / for / hasn't / a / .

   He hasn't been surfing for a long time.

2. hours / been / three / for / chatting / online / We've / !

   _____

3. been / since / Ella's / making / 2011 / films / .

   _____

4. watching / I / been / lately / haven't / movies / any / .

   _____

5. to / running, / but / I / now / love / stopped / I've / running / used / .

   _____

6. haven't / since / rock climbing / 2013 / They / been / .

   _____

**2** Look at Helen's timeline. Complete the questions and answers using the present perfect or the present perfect continuous form of the verbs.

Timeline:
- live in England
- work as a journalist
- 2010  2011  2012  2013  2014  2015  NOW
- study Portuguese
- move to Brazil
- learn to sail

1. **Kay:** Helen, ___have___ you ___been living___ (live) in England?
   **Helen:** No, I _____. I _____ in Brazil.

2. **Kay:** _____ you _____ (sail) for a long time?
   **Helen:** No, I _____. I _____ since 2014.

3. **Kay:** _____ you _____ (work) as a journalist for a long time?
   **Helen:** Not really. I _____ as a journalist since 2013.

4. **Mike:** What _____ Helen _____ doing lately?
   **Kay:** She _____ (work) as a journalist.

5. **Mike:** _____ Helen _____ (study) Spanish?
   **Kay:** No, she _____. She _____ Portuguese.

**3** Rewrite the sentences. Change the present perfect to the present continuous or the present continuous to the present perfect, when possible. Write X if the sentence can't be rewritten.

1. She has never ~~been seeing~~ a Broadway show.

   She has never seen a Broadway show.

2. I've played football for a long time.

   _____

3. Stacy has wanted to buy a car for a long time.

   _____

4. Gavin has been working at the law firm for 10 years.

   _____

5. Ellen has been in Paris since Tuesday.

   _____

**4** Answer the questions. Use your own information.

1. Have you ever studied Russian?

   _____

2. Where have you been studying English?

   _____

3. What have you been doing lately?

   _____

4. What is something you've never done?

   _____

5. How long have you known your best friend?

   _____

Unit 2 | 9

## VOCABULARY  Phrasal verbs about making progress

**1** Complete the sentences with a word from each box. Use the correct verb forms.

| bring | pass | along | up |
| count | set | into | up |
| get | sign | on | up |
| ~~give~~ | turn | on | together |
| keep | | | ~~up~~ |

1. Our team is losing, but they're determined. They won't _____give up_____.
2. The new website has _____ different music fans from all over the world.
3. Marla is so nice that she can _____ with anyone.
4. I helped my grandparents _____ their social networking page.
5. They find it difficult to _____ with all of the latest technology.
6. The organization started small, but it's _____ a global success.
7. Some people worry that they won't be able to _____ their traditions to their grandchildren.
8. Let's _____ to help at the beach clean up.
9. John is always there for you. You can _____ him to help you.

**2** Correct the sentences if needed. Write ✓ if they are already correct.

1. It took 10 minutes to set her new smartphone up. _✓_
2. Millie's so motivated! She's already signed for dance lessons up. _____
3. We've been trying to get with the other team along. _____
4. My dream is to be a writer, and I don't want to give it up. _____
5. That new app has brought some very different people together. _____
6. The organization has a great program to pass used clothing along to people who need it. _____
7. His hobby has turned his career into. _____
8. I don't have time to keep with my social networking up. _____
9. Who can you count for a ride tonight on? _____

**3** Complete the conversation with some of the phrasal verbs from Exercise 1. Use the correct verb forms.

**Andrea:** Have you ¹_____ for the race yet?

**Bill:** No, I haven't. I know it's a great event that ²_____ a lot of people _____, but I don't think I can run that far. I'll ³_____ before I get to the end.

**Andrea:** Bill! Don't ⁴_____ this _____ a big drama! It's just a fun run. I don't run that fast, and I'm doing it. You can ⁵_____ with me, can't you?

**Bill:** I don't know . . .

**Andrea:** Look, you can run with our running group twice a week. We'll ⁶_____ a training program for you. And Ken is training with us, too, you know. I know you ⁷_____ well with him.

**Bill:** Ken's doing the run? Oh, OK. I'll do it.

**Andrea:** Thanks, Bill! I knew I could ⁸_____ you!

## GRAMMAR  Past perfect and past perfect continuous

**1** Read the sentences. Circle the answer that correctly explains each situation.

1. Tina and Mel had been in Africa when the program started.
   a. The program started during their time in Africa. *(circled)*
   b. The program started before they went to Africa.

2. They hadn't been checking their email as often during the program.
   a. They used to check their email regularly before the program.
   b. They didn't use to check their email regularly before the program.

3. The band had been touring since 2010.
   a. They probably toured for a few years and stopped.
   b. They toured and are probably still touring.

4. Sophia had been volunteering at the center for six months.
   a. Sophia is probably still volunteering at the center.
   b. Sophia is probably doing something else now.

5. People had been signing up for the service over the weekend.
   a. It is still the weekend now.
   b. It is some time after the weekend now.

**2** Complete the sentences and questions with the words in parentheses. Use the past perfect continuous.

1. They _had been practicing_ (practice) their new song when the power went out.

2. Tara and Milo _____ (exchange) emails.

3. Their concerts _____ (sell out) quickly.

4. My sister _____ (not study) the piano.

5. We _____ (talk) for hours and hadn't realized the time.

**3** Look at Mai's activities. Complete the sentences with the past perfect and past perfect continuous.

| study dance in Chicago | six years |
| live in Los Angeles | 2011–2013 |
| compete in a television dance show | June 2012 |
| sing and dance in a movie | Summer 2013 |
| move to New York City | October 2013 |
| record an album | 2014 |

1. Mai _had studied_ dance in Chicago for six years.
2. Mai _____ in a dance show before she moved to New York City.
3. She _____ in Los Angeles when she went on TV.
4. Mai _____ in a movie before she moved to New York City.
5. Mai _____ an album in 2014.

**4** Put the words in the correct order to make questions. Answer the questions.

1. in / Mai been / Chicago / studying / dance / Had / ?
   _Had Mai been studying dance in Chicago?_
   _Yes, she had._

2. when / recording / Mai been / she / in / Had / Los Angeles / an album / lived / ?
   _____
   _____

3. to / had / she / moved / Mai been / What / doing / before / New York City / ?
   _____
   _____

4. living / been / Where / 2012 / Mai / in / had / ?
   _____
   _____

## CONVERSATION — Showing concern

**1  Match the phrases to make expressions to show concern.**

1. I'm sorry — d. to hear that.
2. What's the — c. matter?
3. I hope — e. things get better.
4. What's — f. wrong with her?
5. Are you — a. all right?
6. Is there — b. anything I can do?

**2  Use the phrases from Exercise 1 to complete the conversation.**

**Ilona:** Hey, Julio. ¹ *Are you all right?*

**Julio:** I'm OK, I guess.

**Ilona:** No, you're not. You look tired. ² _____

**Julio:** Well, I'm worried about my mother.

**Ilona:** ³ _____

**Julio:** Oh, nothing's wrong with her. In fact, just the opposite. Ever since we got a new puppy, she's been so energetic.

**Ilona:** Who's been energetic? Your mom or the puppy?

**Julio:** Actually, both of them! My mom gets up really early to take the puppy out in the morning. Then, after school, she takes it jogging. And she makes me come with her! That's why I look tired.

**Ilona:** Julio! That's not really a problem, is it?

**Julio:** No, but now she's talking about getting a second dog! I'm going to have to join the track team to keep up.

**Ilona:** That's funny. Well, at least your dog can run. My cat is really overweight. I'm worried about him.

**Julio:** ⁴ _____. ⁵ _____?

**Ilona:** Thanks, but no. We're already doing everything we can to help him eat less and exercise more.

**Julio:** Well, ⁶ _____. And if you ever want to come on a run with us, let me know!

**Ilona:** Thanks!

# READING TO WRITE

**1 Complete Jenny's thank-you email with the correct words.**

| Bye for now | I've attached |
|---|---|
| ~~Hi~~ | Thanks |
| I'm writing to thank you for | Thank you for |

---

**To:** MToth@cup.net
**From:** JennyPalooza@cup.net
**Subject:** Thank you!

¹ _____Hi_____, Ms. Toth,

² _____ being a great art teacher. Since graduating from high school, I've gone to college and I've been studying art. You really motivated me to work harder. Sometimes in class, I look at the other students' work and think they are more talented than me. But then I immediately remember you used to tell me to just be myself and do the work. Gradually, I've been feeling better about my work. ³ _____ that.

I also want to let you know that the oil paints you gave me as a gift have been wonderful! Since I got them, I've been painting much better. I like them more than the watercolors I'd been using.
⁴ _____ so much for them! ⁵ _____ a photo of my latest painting. I hope you like it!

⁶ _____ , Jenny

---

**2 Read the letter in Exercise 1 again. Write the phrases next to each section below.**

A greeting: _____Hi, Ms. Toth_____

A reason for writing: _____

Details: _____

_____

A closing: _____

Sending a photo: _____

**3 Read the letter in Exercise 1 again. Answer the questions.**

1. What was Jenny doing before college?

   _____

2. What phrase in Jenny's email helped you to answer question 1?

   _____

3. How do Jenny's thoughts change during class?

   _____

4. What phrase helped you to answer question 3?

   _____

5. What change has happened for Jenny?

   _____

6. What word explains that this change has happened to Jenny slowly, over time?

   _____

7. Which word explains something that happened after Jenny was given a gift?

   _____

8. What has changed for Jenny since she received the gift?

   _____

# REVIEW UNITS 1–2

**1 Complete the chart.**

| article. | interview | review |
| blogger | motivated | sociable |
| impatient | reporter | |

| Media | People | Personal qualities |
|---|---|---|
| *article* | | |
| | | |
| | | |

**2 Complete each sentence with a word from each box. Use the correct verb forms.**

| count. | along |
| get | into |
| give | on. |
| keep | up |
| set | up |
| turn | up |

1. I used to __count on__ Ella to help me with my homework.
2. I was having trouble _____ with my teammates during the race.
3. His experience writing blog posts _____ a job as a journalist.
4. They got a new laptop, and now they're _____ a new social networking page.
5. Last year, I _____ well with all my classmates.
6. I didn't have enough time to study until I _____ watching television.

**3 Complete the sentences with *would* when possible. If not possible, use *used to*.**

1. I __used to__ listen to hip hop, but now I listen to rock.
2. We _____ watch movies every night, but now we only watch them on weekends.
3. He was so shy, he _____ stay at home every night until he joined our club.
4. Jill _____ ride her bike to school, and now she rides it to work.
5. The organization _____ have a big party every year to thank the volunteers.
6. _____ you listen to the radio every night?

**4 Circle the correct answers.**

1. **Ben:** Who **did** / **was** you **interview** / **interviewed** for the school blog?
   **Max:** I **was interviewing** / **interviewed** Coldplay!
2. The album **was recording** / **was recorded** in the studio. It **wasn't recorded** / **wasn't recording** while the band was on tour.
3. **Mia:** Where **was** / **were** you **watched** / **watching** the news report?
   **Sara:** I **was watching** / **have watched** it online. I **wasn't watching** / **haven't watched** it on television.
4. **Jen:** Who **has been** / **was going** to Rome before?
   **Chris:** Danielle **has been** / **was going** to Rome. I think she **has been** / **went** last May.
5. The interview **was playing** / **has been played** on the radio twice today. But it **didn't post** / **hasn't been posted** on the web page yet.

**5 Correct the sentences.**

1. What have you been ~~do~~ *doing* at the volunteer center?
2. Mara been knowing Lauren since she was five.
3. I have spending three months in Chile this past year.
4. You haven't been post on your web page lately.
5. Elliot was working as a volunteer for two years, but he's running the organization now.
6. They're not having worked late for a long time.

**6** Complete the blog post with the words in parentheses. Use the correct verb forms.

## GETTING READY FOR MY TRIP!
by Emily

I'm really into Mongolian throat singing lately.
I ¹ _had been taking_ (take) singing lessons for about fives years before I learned about Mongolian throat singing.
I ² _____ (not hear) of that kind of singing before. It's an amazing sound because the singer sings two or more sounds at the same time.
Mongolian throat singing ³ _____ (be) around for a long time. Historically, men ⁴ _____ (be) the majority of throat singers, but more women ⁵ _____ (learn) to do it lately.
I ⁶ _____ (work) with a singing coach to practice Mongolian singing, when she told me about a singing camp in Mongolia.
I ⁷ _____ (sign up) right away. It's in Siberia, and most people speak Russian. So, after I ⁸ _____ (sign up) to go, I started taking Russian lessons, too.
I ⁹ _____ (use) my voice a lot lately! I'm so excited for my trip! I leave next month!

**7** Complete the conversation. More than one answer may be possible.

| can't stand | not crazy about |
| crazy about | not that into |
| Is there anything I can do? | ~~What's the matter?~~ |

**Lukas:** Hey, Tatiana. You look upset. ¹ _What's the matter?_

**Tatiana:** Oh, it's nothing important. It's just that Tim got us tickets to go to a car race this weekend.

**Lukas:** Well, that sounds fun!

**Tatiana:** Not for me! I ² _____ car racing! It's so noisy! I told him I wanted to go to the beach.

**Lukas:** Really? I'm ³ _____ car racing!

**Tatiana:** Ugh. I'm ⁴ _____ it. And I'm ⁵ _____ spending my weekend at the race.

**Lukas:** ⁶ _____

**Tatiana:** Yeah, actually there is. Maybe you can go with him to the race instead!

**8** Put the words in the correct order to make sentences. Then use the sentences to complete the conversation.

| her / with / wrong / What's / ? |
| ~~you / Raul / all / right, / Are / ?~~ |
| I / hear / hope / from / you / Well, / her / . |
| into / really / organic farming / She's / . |
| sorry / hear / I'm / that / to / Oh, / . |

**Liana:** ¹ _Are you all right, Raul?_

**Raul:** Not really. I'm worried about my sister.

**Liana:** ² _____

**Raul:** She's in Peru. I haven't heard from her in a while.

**Liana:** What's she been doing there?

**Raul:** ³ _____ So she's been volunteering at a farm in the Amazon jungle. But the last I heard from her, she wasn't feeling well.

**Liana:** ⁴ _____ Well, maybe their power is out or something.

**Raul:** Yeah, maybe.

**Liana:** ⁵ _____

**Raul:** Thanks.

# 3 Planning for the Future

## VOCABULARY  Verbs of the future

**1** Unscramble the verbs used to talk about the future.

1. e o m v  ___move___
2. n a p l  _____
3. w r g o  p u  _____
4. e p k e  n o  _____
5. d e g a t r u a  _____
6. e c m b e o  _____
7. d e n  p u  _____
8. t r i p e c d  _____

**2** Complete the sentences with the phrases from Exercise 1. Use the correct verb forms.

1. Jason is good at art. I ___predict___ he'll study painting in college.
2. I really enjoy playing the guitar. I have to _____ practicing so I can play in a band.
3. After I _____ to London, I hope to get a job at a start-up company.
4. Ellen wants to take a year off and travel after she _____ from high school.
5. He's not _____ to work for a company after college. He wants to start his own business!
6. My nine-year-old sister loves animals. She can't wait to _____ and become a veterinarian.
7. If you don't work toward your goals, you'll _____ doing nothing.
8. He studied music for many years before he _____ a professional musician.

**3** Complete Julian's email with some of the expressions from Exercise 1. Use the correct verb forms.

To: Mariano_M@cambridge.edu
From: JulianCompU@cambridge.edu
Subject: Hello!

Dear Mr. Mariano,

How are you? I haven't talked to you since I ¹ ___graduated___ from high school! I wanted to update you on what I've been doing and what I'm ² _____ for the future.

As you know, I'm in college and I've been studying computers. It's difficult, but I will ³ _____ studying until computer science ⁴ _____ easier for me!

I ⁵ _____ that I will graduate in four more years. After that, I think I will ⁶ _____ to San Francisco and will probably ⁷ _____ working for a computer game company.

You know, computer games have been a big part of my life. When I was little, I told myself, "When I ⁸ _____, I will make games that kids love to play." And now, I'm working on that goal! Anyway, I wanted you to know that I really appreciated your computer class in high school!

Sincerely,

Julian

**4** Write statements about your future. Use the words in parentheses and your own information.

1. (plan)
   _I plan on visiting a new country every year._
   _____

2. (become)
   _____

3. (keep on)
   _____

4. (end up)
   _____

## GRAMMAR  Future review

**1  Complete the chart.**

| will for predictions | be going to for planned actions and events |
|---|---|
| 1. What flight _____ Charlotte take? She**'ll** take the flight from London. She ___*won't*___ take the one from Glasgow. | 2. Who _____ she _____ visit? She _____ visit her cousins. She **isn't going to** visit her college friends. |
| **Present continuous for planned actions and events** | **Simple present for scheduled future events** |
| 3. Which suitcase _____ she **taking** with her? She _____ the green suitcase. She **isn't taking** the brown one. | 4. What **does** she ___*plan*___ to see? She _____ to see the Met and a show on Broadway. She **doesn't** _____ to see Ellis Island. |

**2  Complete the sentences about Jorge's future plans. Circle the correct forms of the verbs.**

1. Next weekend, Jorge **(is going to)** / **going** graduate from college. He **isn't going to** / **isn't going** keep on taking classes.

2. After graduating, Jorge **is going to plan** / **plans** to have a party at his house.

3. Jorge **will have** / **is having** a fun graduation party next weekend.

4. Next month, Jorge **will go** / **is going** to Peru.

5. Jorge **will** / **plans** to work at a non-profit organization in Peru.

6. He thinks he **will go** / **is going** to law school when he returns from Peru.

**3  Use the chart to complete the questions and answers with future tenses. More than one answer may be possible.**

|  | Planned actions | Planned events | Predictions |
|---|---|---|---|
| **James** | spend a month (August) in Paris | study at a French language school | travel in Europe in the fall |
| **Rita** | live in New York July – August | intern at a magazine | get hired by magazine in September |

1. Q: Where ___*is*___ James ___*planning*___ to go in August?
   A: He'___*s planning*___ to go to Paris.

2. Q: What _____ James _____ in Paris?
   A: He's _____ French at a language school.

3. Q: What _____ James _____ in the fall?
   A: He _____ in Europe.

4. Q: When _____ Rita _____ in New York?
   A: She _____ there from July to August.

5. Q: What _____ she _____ to do there?
   A: She _____ to intern at a magazine.

6. Q: What _____ she _____ after that?
   A: She _____ by the magazine.

**4  Answer the questions about a friend.**

1. Q: What is your friend planning to do tomorrow?
   A: _____

2. Q: What will your friend do next weekend?
   A: _____

3. Q: What will your friend do next year?
   A: _____

## VOCABULARY  Achievements

**1** Complete the phrases. Then match the pictures with the phrases.

| 1. | win | an award | c |
|---|---|---|---|
| 2. |  | a business |  |
| 3. | do |  |  |
| 4. |  | a record |  |
| 5. | support |  |  |
| 6. |  | a million dollars |  |
| 7. |  | a project |  |
| 8. |  | famous |  |

a.
b.
c.
d.
e.
f.
g.
h.

**2** Answer the questions with the phrases from Exercise 1.

1. Which three achievements can relate to sports?

   _____, _____, and _____

2. Which three achievements most likely relate to a business?

   _____, _____, and _____

3. Which two achievements most likely help people?

   _____ and _____

**3** Complete the sentences with the correct form of phrases from Exercise 1. Then check (✓) if the sentences are true for you.

|  | True |
|---|---|
| 1. I think __winning an award__ for something you've done well is the best feeling. |  |
| 2. I want to _____ so I can support my family. It would be nice not to worry about money. |  |
| 3. I think that when people _____, they don't have any privacy. But it is still great because everyone knows who you are! |  |
| 4. If I _____, I can make the company's rules. |  |
| 5. I think people should _____ more often. There are always places to clean up or community projects that need help. |  |
| 6. I think anyone can _____. These days, you can raise money online to fund anything, even a movie you'd like to make! |  |
| 7. I want to work for an organization that _____. I think it's important to work locally to improve things. |  |
| 8. I think that if you practice and work hard, it's possible to _____ in any sport. But you have to really want to do it. |  |

**4** Complete the questions with some of the phrases from Exercise 1. Then write answers that are true for you.

1. **Q:** Who do you think deserves to win __an award__?
   **A:** _I think Leonardo DiCaprio deserves to win an_
   _award for donating money to save the oceans._
   _____
   _____

2. **Q:** Which of your friends do you think will become _____? Why?
   **A:** _____

3. **Q:** What kind of business would you like to _____?
   **A:** _____

4. **Q:** What kind of _____ work would you like to do?
   **A:** _____

5. Q: What record would you like to _____?
   A: _____

6. Q: If you _____ a million dollars, how will you spend it?
   A: _____

## GRAMMAR  Future continuous and future perfect

**1  Complete the chart.**

| Use future continuous to describe something in progress in the future. | |
|---|---|
| 1. Who _will_ be _supporting_ the race on Saturday? Our club _____ _____ the race on Saturday. | 2. _____ Donny _____ volunteering at the beach clean up? No, he _____. But I will. |

| Use future perfect to describe something that is going to be finished at a certain time in the future. | |
|---|---|
| 3. What _will_ your team _have_ developed by next year? We _____ _____ a community garden. | 4. _____ Everett _____ a business by next year? Yes, he _____. |

**2  Change the sentences. Change the present continuous to the future continuous or future perfect.**

1. Alex is volunteering with Kim next week.
   _Alex will be volunteering with Kim next week._

2. They're collecting a million dollars by this time next month.
   _____
   _____

3. They're using the money they collect to do a community project.
   _____
   _____

4. By 2020, the project is helping over 1,000 children.
   _____
   _____

5. Rachel thinks the organization is winning an award for community service by 2017.
   _____
   _____

6. They're supporting community projects in Haiti.
   _____
   _____

**3  Answer the questions with your own ideas. Use the future continuous or future perfect.**

1. Which of your friends will have made a million dollars in the next 10 years?
   _I think my friend Zack will have made a_
   _million dollars in the next 10 years. He's very_
   _hard-working._
   _____
   _____

2. Which of your friends do you think will be helping his/her community in the next two years?
   _____
   _____

3. Which of your friends will have traveled the most by 2025?
   _____
   _____

4. Which of your friends do you think will have started a business?
   _____
   _____

5. What will you be doing in 10 years?
   _____
   _____

## CONVERSATION — Expressing cause and effect

**1. Circle the correct answers.**

1. The neighborhood created the community garden **as a result / (so that)** people would have access to fresh fruit and vegetables.
2. The shoe company has been donating 10 percent of its profits to charity, and **because of / consequently** their sales have gone up.
3. Pollution from plastic bags in the ocean has decreased **so that / thanks to** the new law that bans them.
4. Terry was able to save money for a new guitar **because of / since** his part-time job.
5. **Since / Consequently**, the number of people donating to the charity has increased, more projects are getting funded.
6. The benefit concert was a huge success, and **so that / as a result**, the class has earned enough money for a graduation party.

**2 Complete the conversation with the phrases from Exercise 1. More than one answer may be possible.**

Luis: Hi, Kathryn. ¹ _____Thanks to_____ you, our after-school club will be getting two new laptops!

Kathryn: Really? What did I do?

Luis: ² _____ your article in the paper, some local businesses started a donation program. ³ _____, they donated enough money for us to buy two new computers. Even the Senior Center donated!

Kathryn: Wow! You know, ⁴ _____ they donated to us, maybe we should help them. We could take the laptops to the Senior Center and help the seniors to send emails and talk to their families. You know, do something nice for them ⁵ _____ they know we appreciate what they did for us.

Luis: That's a fantastic idea!

# READING TO WRITE

**1 Complete Michelle's opinion essay with the correct words.**

For paragraph B:

| consequently | ~~For one thing~~ |
| inevitably | what's more |

For paragraph C:

| in addition | obviously |
| surely | therefore |

## Should soft drinks be sold at School?

by Michelle Leto

A What do you drink at lunch? Many schools in the United States have food and drinks for sale at lunchtime. Many schools have vending machines that sell soda. Personally, I don't think sodas or soft drinks with sugar in them should be sold at schools. Everyone knows by now that too much sugar isn't healthy.

B Why is sugar bad? [1] _For one thing_ , sugar has a lot of calories, but it does not provide any nutrients — the good things the body needs to stay healthy. [2] _____, the empty calories in sugar make people gain weight. [3] _____, eating sugar gives people a burst of energy at first, but then it makes them feel tired. Almost [4] _____, people then want to eat even more sugar.

C Research shows that people weigh more today than they did 50 years ago. [5] _____ to eating too much sugar, this is because people are not exercising enough. This is [6] _____ not healthy. Everyone can see that! [7] _____ something could be done to help get people interested in exercising. [8] _____, I think schools should require an hour of exercise every morning to music that students get to choose.

D Some people think that students should be able to make their own choices. I agree with that for some things. For example, I think it's important for students to be able to choose classes that prepare them for their chosen careers.

E But schools are meant to educate. So I think it's important to teach students to make better choices about their health.

**2 Read the article in Exercise 1 again. Write the paragraph letters next to each section below.**

___ A paragraph with arguments in favor

___ A conclusion

___ An introduction

___ , ___ Paragraphs with arguments against

**3 Read the article in Exercise 1 again. Answer the questions.**

1. What does Michelle use to get the reader's attention?
   _____
   _____

2. What reasons does Michelle give against sugar?
   _____
   _____

3. What does Michelle say that schools should do to help students get more exercise?
   _____
   _____

4. What does Michelle think students should be allowed to choose?
   _____
   _____

Unit 3 | 21

# 4 What's Cooking?

## VOCABULARY  Cooking verbs

**1** Find eight more cooking verbs. Then label the pictures.

| I | L | E | J | L | P | Z | K | W | S |
|---|---|---|---|---|---|---|---|---|---|
| B | F | W | S | R | O | A | S | T | P |
| E | R | D | G | R | I | L | L | R | L |
| S | Y | B | O | I | L | Z | W | N | J |
| L | B | P | C | H | I | V | Z | N | M |
| I | A | F | H | I | O | X | G | M | I |
| C | K | U | O | V | K | X | R | Y | X |
| E | E | W | P | S | J | N | A | C | U |
| M | I | U | J | I | T | Z | T | B | I |
| V | Q | T | H | H | K | T | E | M | T |

1. _roast_
2. _____
3. _____
4. _____
5. _____
6. _____
7. _____
8. _____
9. _____

**2** Complete Justin's email with some of the words from Exercise 1. Use the simple past.

Hi Wanda,

I am having a great time at chef school! It's more difficult than I expected, but I'm learning a lot. Did you know that we had a whole lesson just learning how to ¹ _boil_ water? And then we spent an entire week just learning knife skills, such as how to ² _____ meat and how to ³ _____ onions into little pieces. That lesson made me cry! Ha ha!

It's funny. I thought I knew the basics of how to cook, but since coming here, I've already learned so much! For instance, I now know why the skin turns brown on top when you ⁴ _____ a chicken, and why the dough rises when you ⁵ _____ bread. Yesterday, we learned how to ⁶ _____ potatoes. I mean, make French fries! That was so much harder than you'd think. But I still like to ⁷ _____ best. Cooking burgers outdoors is my idea of fun. Hey, maybe when I come home I can cook for you and your friends. That would be fun!

Write back soon,

Justin

**3** Answer the questions with your own information.

1. Which cooking activities from Exercise 1 are your favorites?

   _I like baking cookies and cakes._
   _____

2. What is your favorite way to prepare chicken?
   _____

3. What is the easiest way to cook something?
   _____

4. What is the most difficult way to cook something?
   _____

## GRAMMAR  First conditional review; zero conditional

**1** Check (✓) if the sentence uses first conditional or zero conditional.

|  | First conditional (possible results) | Zero conditional (always true) |
|---|---|---|
| 1. When you bake a cake, you need to measure the ingredients carefully. |  | ✓ |
| 2. If we don't clean up after the picnic, mice will come. |  |  |
| 3. You don't have to add salt, unless you like really salty food. |  |  |
| 4. If Tom eats shrimp, he gets a rash. |  |  |
| 5. I don't want a slice of cake, unless you want to share one. |  |  |
| 6. When it's been a cold winter, the price of oranges goes up. |  |  |

**2** Correct the first conditional sentences.

1. If I ~~will~~ eat a hamburger for dinner, I won't eat dessert afterward.

2. If we eat Chinese food tonight, we use chopsticks.

3. I not eat dessert at the restaurant, unless they have chocolate cake.

4. If she eats too many cookies this afternoon, her stomach hurt.

5. You want to have some of this delicious pizza, unless you don't like tomatoes.

**3** Correct the zero conditional sentences.

1. When you boil an egg too fast, it ₐturn grey inside. *(will)*

2. If you won't use enough water to boil rice, it becomes too sticky.

3. Meat won't cook through evenly when you will put it on the grill cold from the refrigerator.

4. When your stomach will hurt, you can drink some mint tea.

5. You can take away some of the bad smell if you will rinse fresh garlic under water before using it.

**4** Complete the conversation. When possible, use the first conditional. If the zero conditional is needed, write X.

**Ellen:** Hi, Rafe. What are you cooking?

**Rafe:** I'm going to cook this fish. I can't decide if I want to fry it or grill it, though.

**Ellen:** Well, when you fry fish, the whole house ¹ _X_ smells.

**Rafe:** That's true. But if I open the window, it ² _____ smell.

**Ellen:** Well, not as much.

**Rafe:** If I grill the fish outside, the house ³ _____ smell.

**Ellen:** Yes, but the grill takes a long time to heat up. You ⁴ _____ need to heat it up now if you want to eat dinner by seven.

**Rafe:** Oh, I forgot about that. Do you think there's enough time?

**Ellen:** I'm not sure. Maybe we should just go out to dinner at the Seaside Café.

**Rafe:** That fancy new place?! If you want to eat at the Seaside Café, you ⁵ _____ need to make a reservation two weeks ahead of time! Besides, I can't go unless you pay. I spent all my money on the fish!

**Ellen:** You know, if we bake the fish in the oven, it ⁶ _____ take very long.

## VOCABULARY Adjectives describing food

**1** Find nine more adjectives that describe food.

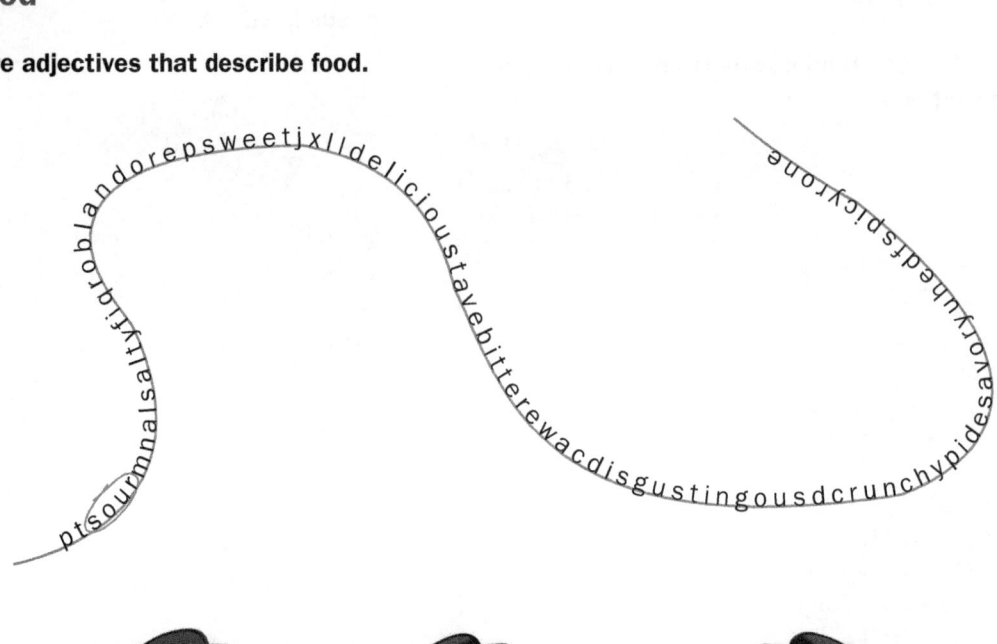

*(word snake contains: sour, salty, bland, sweet, delicious, bitter, disgusting, crunchy, spicy)*

**2** Circle the food or drink the first word best describes.

| | | |
|---|---|---|
| 1. sour | a. banana | b. lemon |
| 2. sweet | a. candy | b. French fries |
| 3. bitter | a. milk | b. coffee |
| 4. crunchy | a. steak | b. tortilla chips |
| 5. salty | a. cake | b. potato chips |
| 6. spicy | a. chili peppers | b. grapes |
| 7. delicious | a. celery | b. pizza |
| 8. disgusting | a. fried spiders | b. bread |
| 9. savory | a. burgers | b. strawberries |
| 10. bland | a. crackers | b. nachos |

**3** Complete the sentences. Use some of the words from Exercise 2. More than one answer may be possible.

1. John broke a tooth when he was eating ____*crunchy*____ peanuts.
2. Helen's stomach hurts. She should eat some _____ food, like rice or toast.
3. I like to eat curry if it's not too _____. But sometimes the flavor is just too hot!
4. My sister can't cook. One time, she made chicken noodle soup and added chocolate to it. It was _____! No one could eat it.
5. My mother only drinks coffee with milk and sugar. She says it's too _____ otherwise.
6. In Japan, a lot of people say sushi is the most _____ food. That's why they serve it on special occasions.
7. I'm always thirsty after I eat in a restaurant. Restaurant food is so _____.
8. I usually eat something _____ like ham and eggs for breakfast instead of something _____ like pancakes.
9. Mom forgot to add sugar to the lemonade, and it was so _____!

**4** Answer the questions. Use your own ideas.

1. What is your favorite salty food? _____
2. What is your favorite sweet food? _____
3. What two flavors do you like to combine? _____
4. What food do you think is disgusting? _____

24 | Unit 4

## GRAMMAR — Second conditional review

**1** Complete the chart with the second conditional to describe imaginary situations and possible consequences.

| Yes/No questions |
| --- |
| 1. _Would_ you order fried *chapulines* _if_ they _____were_____ on the menu? |
| No, I _wouldn't_. |
| I _wouldn't_ eat them _if_ you paid me. |
| 2. _____ someone offered them to you, _____ you eat insects? |
| Yes, I _____. |
| No, _____ someone offered them to me, I _____ eat them. |

| Wh- questions |
| --- |
| 3. _____ you had to give up a favorite food, which one _____ you give up? |
| I _____ probably give up hamburgers. |
| 4. What food _____ you try _____ you were in Australia? |
| I _____ probably try fried alligator. |

**2** Circle the correct answers.

**Elena:** Hey, Chris. ①(**If**)/ **Would** somebody offered you fried alligator tail, **were / would** you eat it?

**Chris:** I probably ²**was / would**.

**Elena:** Ew! Really?

**Chris:** Yeah. I ³**were / would** try anything once.

**Elena:** OK. ⁴**If / Would** you **was / were** really hungry, **if / would** you eat horse meat?

**Chris:** Hmm. I don't know. Oh, I probably ⁵**did / would**.

**Elena:** OK. ⁶**Did / Would** you still eat horse meat **if / were** you met the horse first?

**Chris:** You got me. No, ⁷**if / would** I met the horse first, then I probably **weren't / wouldn't**.

**3** Write second conditional questions with the information in the chart.

| | Imaginary situation | Possible consequence |
| --- | --- | --- |
| 1. | we / be / Japan | what / we / eat |
| 2. | you / can learn to cook / anything | what / it / be |
| 3. | Tina / have to give up / bread or rice | which / she / give up |
| | **Possible consequence** | **Imaginary situation** |
| 4. | Aldo / eat jellyfish | he / be alone on an island |
| 5. | they / eat raw meat | they / have no other choice |

1. _If we were in Japan, what would we eat?_
2. _____
3. _____
4. _____
5. _____

**4** Write the questions another way. Then answer the questions with your own information.

1. Would you eat *fugu* if it were offered to you?

   **Q:** _If it were offered to you, would you eat fugu?_
   **A:** _No, I wouldn't._

2. If you were to cook a meal to impress someone, what would you cook?

   **Q:** _____
   **A:** _____

3. If you could try any new food, what would you try?

   **Q:** _____
   **A:** _____

4. If you could eat as much of a food as you'd like, what would you eat?

   **Q:** _____
   **A:** _____

## CONVERSATION  Cooking instructions

**1. Circle the correct answers.**

1. When you use just a little bit of something, it's called **a pinch** / **a simmer**.
2. You can use a spoon to **simmer** / **stir** something.
3. You can **pinch** / **pour** something liquid, such as milk or oil.
4. When you **pour** / **simmer** sauce, it is not as hot as when you boil it.
5. "**First of all**"/ "**Then add**" is the phrase that comes before the step you do at the beginning.
6. If you pour some milk onto cereal, you are **adding** /**simmering** it to the cereal.

**2 Complete the conversation with the expressions from Exercise 1.**

**Ernie:** Hey, Jack. Would you like some breakfast? I'm going to cook some eggs.

**Jack:** Why don't you make an omelet?

**Ernie:** I've never cooked an omelet before, but I can try.

**Jack:** It's easy. I'll tell you how to do it. ¹*First of all*, you need to take the skin off the tomato. ² _____ it in hot water for a few minutes. Then the skin comes off easily. Then you can chop it.

**Ernie:** OK. Now what?

**Jack:** Next, you need to beat about four eggs. ³ _____ the tomatoes to the eggs. I like to add some herbs and a ⁴ _____ of salt and pepper. Gently ⁵ _____ it with a wide spoon.

**Ernie:** We have parsley and chives, so I'll add those herbs.

**Jack:** Great. Put some oil into a pan and heat it up. When the pan is hot, ⁶ _____ the egg mixture into it.

**Ernie:** Got it. How does this look?

**Jack:** Use a fork to lift the cooked edges up and let the egg liquid run underneath. That's right. And we're done!

# READING TO WRITE

**1 Complete the sentences with the correct words.**

| a great deal of | a lot of | not enough |
| not much | so | such |
| too much | | |

1. If you put ___too much___ water in the pot, it will spill over when it boils.

2. What did you put in this stew? It is _____ delicious!

3. This tastes bland! There are _____ herbs in it.

4. I don't think we need any more pepper in the soup. There's _____ it in the soup already.

5. Can you pass the salt, please? I like _____ salt on my French fries.

6. This is _____ good bread! You are really good at baking.

7. This is a healthy cookie recipe. There's _____ sugar in it.

**2 Complete the text with some of the phrases from Exercise 1.**

## My Grandmother's Signature Dish

by Iris

My grandmother is from Portugal, near Spain. Every year around the holidays, she makes our family's signature dish: *Bacalhau*. It is a salted, dried cod fish that is served in many different ways, often with potatoes. People say there are 365 different ways to prepare *bacalhau* – one for each day of the year. It is ¹ ___such___ a common dish in Europe and places like the Dominican Republic and Puerto Rico. The dish originated in Norway, where the cod fish is found.

To make the dish, you fry the fish in a pan with some onions and garlic. You add a pinch of salt and pepper, but not ² _____ salt! There is ³ _____ salt in the fish already.

Then you spread some oil in a pan. You put chopped potatoes, carrots, and cabbage in the bottom of the pan. Then you put the cod fish and onions and garlic on top of it. You bake it in the oven for about 30 minutes. To serve it, you put sliced boiled eggs and olives on top. It is ⁴ _____ delicious!

There are ⁵ _____ variations; some people add chickpeas (garbanzos) or cream. You should try them all!

**3 Read the text again. Answer the questions.**

1. What is Iris's grandmother's signature dish?

2. What are the main ingredients?

3. How is it made?

4. What are some variations?

5. Where else is the dish eaten?

# REVIEW UNITS 3–4

**1** Write the words next to the definitions.

| bake | end up | predict |
|---|---|---|
| bland | fry | spicy |
| chop | keep on | |
| delicious | mix | |

1. To arrive somewhere without a plan. *end up*
2. To say what will happen in the future. _____
3. To cut into small pieces or cubes. _____
4. _____ food with little flavor is the opposite of _____ food.
5. To cook something using hot oil in a pan on a stovetop. _____
6. To cook something, such as a cake or cookies, using dry heat in the oven. _____
7. To continue and not stop or give up. _____
8. To combine different things together. _____
9. A lively flavor that is often called "hot." _____

**2** Complete the sentences with a word from each box.

| break | an award |
|---|---|
| develop | a business |
| do | the community |
| start | a project |
| support | a record |
| win | volunteer work |

1. Sue has donated money to fund the new playground. She wants to *support the community*.
2. Ralph has been running a lot, and his time is faster than everyone's. He's probably going to _____ in the next race.
3. They plan to _____ that will bring fresh water to the area.
4. I just think that everyone should _____ _____ at some point in their life. It feels good to help people.
5. Elon says he will _____ when he graduates from school. He wants to make a lot of money.
6. Carol sold the most houses this year, so she is going to _____.

**3** Look at the pictures and complete the puzzle. Then complete the sentences about Mia by unscrambling the letters in the grey boxes.

Mia will probably _____ being a chef.

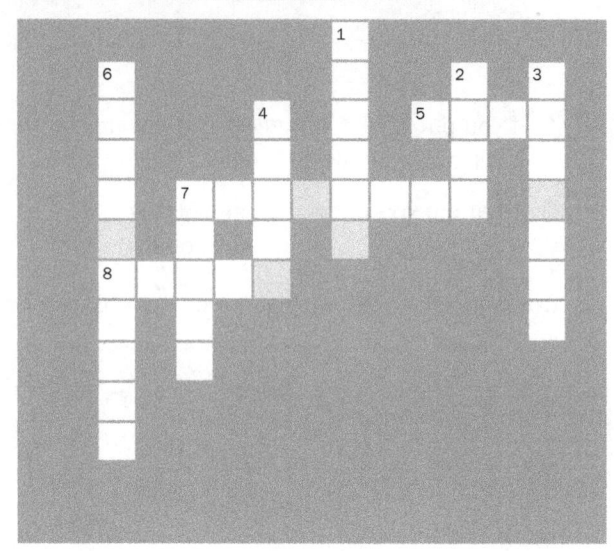

**across**
5. 7.  8.

**down**
1. 2.  3. 
4.  6.  7.

**4** Put the words in the correct order to make sentences. Write each sentence two ways.

1. you / eat fugu / should / to take / if / you / like / risks / .

   *If you like to take risks, you should eat fugu.*

   *You should eat fugu,* _____

2. you / like / the jellyfish / don't / unless / order / unusual tastes / .

   _____

   _____

28 | Review 2

3. eat / when / your breath / you / garlic / smells / .

   _____

   _____

4. will be / you add / unless / a lot of / spices / this chili / bland / .

   _____

   _____

5. be bitter / add / if / will / you / sugar / don't / the coffee / .

   _____

   _____

6. a Japanese restaurant / we go / when / eat / won't / Steve / sushi / to / .

   _____

   _____

**5** Look at Anya's Life Plan list. Then complete the questions and answers about her plans. Use *will*, *going to*, the future continuous, and future perfect.

*My Life Plan, April 2016:*

*June 2016 — Graduate from college*
*July 2016 — Start a website*
*July to August 2016 — Save money from summer job*
*September 2016 — Move to Austin, get job*
*September 2016 — Volunteer at animal shelter*
*January 2017 — Develop a project to help dogs*

1. Where _is_ Anya _going to move_ ?

   She _is going to move to_ Austin.

2. Where _____ she _____ in September?

   She's _____ at an animal shelter.

3. _____ she _____ from her summer job by September?

   Yes, _____.

4. What _____ she _____ by July 2016?

   She _____ a website.

5. What _____ she _____ in January of 2017?

   She _____ a project to help dogs.

**6** Complete the conversations with the correct phrases.

| add | because of | since |
| a pinch of | ~~first of all~~ | so that |
| as a result | let it simmer | |

1. **A:** How do I sign up for this volunteer program?

   **B:** _First of all_ , you need to fill out this application online.

2. **A:** How much sugar should I add to your coffee?

   **B:** Just _____ sugar, please.

3. **A:** What do I do after I've added the chicken to the soup?

   **B:** Turn down the heat and then _____ for at least half an hour.

4. **A:** Why isn't Mitchell making limeade for the picnic?

   **B:** He said limes cost too much this year _____ of the bad weather!

5. **A:** Why isn't Jeanne coming to the party this weekend?

   **B:** She isn't coming _____ her new job. She has to work on weekends now.

6. **A:** I'm making hot chocolate. It's almost done.

   **B:** _____ just a drop of vanilla at the end. It really improves the flavor.

7. **A:** Why isn't Helen eating meat?

   **B:** She's stopped eating it _____ she watched that documentary about farms.

8. **A:** Are you taking classes next fall?

   **B:** Yes, I am. I changed my schedule at work _____ I can take two classes.

# 5 Fame and Fortune

**VOCABULARY** Verbs expressing opinion

**1 Unscramble the words to make verbs to express opinions.**

1. E T H A — *hate*
2. R E D A I M — _____
3. L E F E — _____
4. N O M R E M D C E — _____
5. P E F E R R — _____
6. P E T E R C S — _____
7. P E T E R C A P A I — _____
8. K H I N T — _____
9. K E D S I I L — _____

**2 Circle the correct answers.**

1. Jack never watches horror movies. He _____ documentaries.
   a. thinks   b. (prefers)   c. hates

2. Eliza _____ action movies. She thinks most of them are about special effects and not an actual story.
   a. hates   b. recommends   c. feels

3. Although Ben dislikes singing in musicals, he _____ the talented actors who perform in them.
   a. dislikes   b. prefers   c. appreciates

4. I _____ that it is more difficult to do comedy than dramatic acting.
   a. admire   b. hate   c. think

5. I _____ watching movies before I've read the movie reviews. I like to form my own opinions.
   a. prefer   b. admire   c. respect

6. I _____ actors who do their own stunts. It's exciting to watch an actor who has learned to ride a motorcycle or jump from a building.
   a. dislike   b. feel   c. respect

7. Mary _____ famous actors, but she wouldn't want to be one.
   a. admires   b. thinks   c. prefers

8. Jim _____ people who star in reality shows only want fame.
   a. prefers   b. thinks   c. hates

**3 Unscramble the questions. Then answer the questions using the words from Exercise 1 and your own information.**

1. about / you / How / usually / documentaries / feel / do / ?

   *How do you usually feel about documentaries?*
   *I appreciate the people who make documentaries.*
   *They call attention to important issues.*

2. kind / prefer / do / of / movies / What / you / ?

   _____
   _____

3. celebrity / admire / the most / do / Which / you / ?

   _____
   _____

4. friends / would / to / What / recommend / movie / you / your / ?

   _____
   _____

5. dislike / do / reality TV shows / What / you / about / ?

   _____
   _____

30 | Unit 5

## GRAMMAR  Defining and non-defining relative clauses

**1** Match the defining relative clauses with their nouns. Write *who, which, that, where,* or *whose.*

| Noun | Defining relative clause |
|---|---|
| 1. Movies __c__ | a. _____ phones were hacked were angry. |
| 2. The contestants ____ | b. _____ I read last week was also a movie. |
| 3. The house ____ | c. __that__ don't use professional actors are interesting. |
| 4. The celebrities ____ | d. _____ are on game shows must be nervous. |
| 5. The book ____ | e. _____ the movie was filmed is now a museum. |

**2** Rewrite the sentences. Add the non-defining relative clause in parentheses. Use *who, which, where,* or *whose,* and commas.

1. Leonardo DiCaprio donated $2 million to the marine conservation group Oceans 5. (starred in *Titanic*)

   *Leonardo DiCaprio, who starred in Titanic, donated $2 million to the marine conservation group Oceans 5.*

2. Mark Zuckerberg donated millions to the Newark, New Jersey, school system. (his personal wealth is over $30 billion)

   _____

   _____

3. Potcake Place is a charity in the Turks and Caicos Islands. (its goal is to rescue a breed of dog called the "potcake")

   _____

   _____

4. Brad Pitt's charity, the Make It Right Foundation, is based in New Orleans, Louisiana. (he owns a house there)

   _____

   _____

5. Malala Yousafzai donated $50,000 to schools in Gaza. (won the Nobel Peace Prize)

   _____

   _____

6. Doctors Without Borders is helping to care for sick people in Western Africa. (operates in over 70 countries)

   _____

   _____

7. Fashion blogger Tavi Gevinson starred in a Broadway play. (her online magazine for teen girls gets 3.5 million hits per month)

   _____

   _____

8. The African Library Project works to develop libraries in English-speaking countries such as Sierra Leone. (less than 25 percent of adult women are able to read there)

   _____

   _____

**3** Correct the sentences. Correct punctuation, if needed.

1. My friend Elizabeth, ~~which~~ *who* volunteers at the hospital, wants to be a doctor.

2. A "philanthropist" is someone whose donates money to charities and organizations to help others.

3. My cousin's band where plays really cool music got to open for Arcade Fire in 2015.

4. It seems like the companies, who have a social mission, are more successful than those who just want to make a lot of money.

5. Captain Paul Watson whose once belonged to Greenpeace founded the Sea Shepherd Conservation Society to protect marine life.

6. We went to Mavericks Beach, that the annual big wave surfing contest takes place.

Unit 5 | 31

## VOCABULARY   Adverbs of degree

**1** Circle seven more adverbs of degree. Write them in order on the chart.

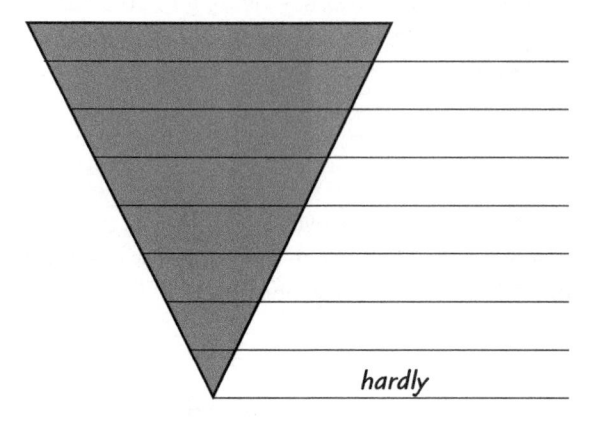

*hardly ~~barely~~ slightly extremely ~~eps~~ nearly ~~algpu~~ pretty ~~nvyty~~ fairly ~~hijkl~~ perfectly ~~lyuso~~ absolutely ~~vps~~*

[inverted pyramid chart with "hardly" at the bottom]

**2** Write the words from Exercise 1 that have the same meaning.

1. very well, completely _____ _____
2. very much, really _____
3. somewhat, kind of _____, _____
4. almost _____
5. just a little _____
6. barely at all _____

**3** Put the words in the correct order to make sentences that use adverbs of degree.

1. sure / sold out / the / yet / pretty / concert / I'm / hasn't / .

   *I'm pretty sure the concert hasn't sold out yet.*

2. about / I'm / new / crazy / Lorde's / absolutely / album / .

   _____

3. hardly / speaks / I / him / can / softly, / so / hear / Carl / .

   _____

4. have / I / fairly / open / who / door / good idea / a / left / the / .

   _____

5. my old one / fine / smartphone / I / don't / when / perfectly / need / works / a / new / .

   _____

6. too / much / felt / eating / dinner / ill / after / slightly / for / We / .

   _____

7. to / practice / become / successful / hard / extremely / Musicians / .

   _____

8. nearly / Jen / was / she / fell / at / when / finish line / the / .

   _____

**4** Read the pairs of sentences. Rewrite the first sentence in each pair using an adverb of degree. More than one answer may be possible.

1. Haley came very close to getting a role in that new movie. But Susanne got it instead.

   *Haley nearly got a role in that new movie.*

2. Ken sang the song the first time. He sang it exactly right!

   _____

3. He would've made the goal if it had been kicked more to the right. It was very close.

   _____

4. Hank looked scared during the movie. I don't think he'll ever go see another one.

   _____

5. I'm convinced that I want to have a career in marine conservation. I have made my decision.

   _____

## GRAMMAR  Tag questions

**1  Match the sentences with the tag questions.**

1. You watched the game last night, __b__
2. You were at the café yesterday, ____
3. You'd donate money if you could, ____
4. You haven't been to Hollywood, ____
5. You'll clean up the kitchen, ____

a. have you?
b. didn't you?
c. won't you?
d. weren't you?
e. wouldn't you?

**2  Add tag questions.**

1. That game was pretty close, __wasn't it__?
2. I like listening to music that makes me feel good, _____?
3. You think watching the news is boring, _____?
4. Tim almost fell asleep during the movie, _____?
5. You haven't seen Bruno Mars in concert, _____?
6. Traffic is moving extremely slowly in downtown Los Angeles, _____?
7. That's the actress who was in that movie, _____?

**3  Correct the tag questions. More than one answer may be possible.**

*weren't*
1. The tickets were expensive, ~~haven't~~ they?
2. This show is funny, doesn't it?
3. Kids shouldn't play video games so often, aren't they?
4. This is the way to the museum, can it?
5. They really like all of the *Star Wars* movies, should they?
6. Uma Thurman's father is a college professor, OK?
7. Bill Murray often plays jokes on ordinary people, would he?
8. Adam Levine from Maroon 5 does yoga, can't he?

**4  Write questions. Use the tag questions and your own information.**

1. (isn't it)  *It's Monday today, isn't it?*

2. (haven't they) _____

3. (weren't we) _____

4. (doesn't it) _____

5. (right) _____

## CONVERSATION — Making a point

**1. Circle the correct answers.**

1. **A:** This movie is going to be boring, isn't it?
   **B:** _____ It might be interesting.
   a. Of course.   b. Not necessarily!

2. **A:** If everybody had to do some volunteer work, people might be nicer to each other.
   **B:** _____ And it might make people feel a sense of community.
   a. Not necessarily!   b. That's a good point.

3. **A:** The books are always better than the movies, right?
   **B:** _____ The actors are never like you picture the characters.
   a. As far as I'm concerned.   b. Of course!

4. **A:** Want to take some more golf lessons?
   **B:** _____, those are the last lessons I want to take!
   a. As far as I'm concerned   b. You're absolutely right

5. **A:** Do you think celebrities support charities for publicity or because they care?
   **B:** _____ some of them do it because they care.
   a. Not necessarily   b. It seems to me that

6. **A:** I bet I won't like some of this music 10 years from now.
   **B:** _____. People's taste in music can change.
   a. As far as I'm concerned   b. You're absolutely right

**2 Circle the correct answers.**

1. **Bill:** I'm excited about the sci-fi conference! Hey, are you wearing that? ¹**It seems to me that** / **Not necessarily** it would be better if we wore similar costumes.
   **Ted:** ²**As far as I'm concerned.** / **You're absolutely right**. That's why I got you a costume like mine!

2. **Esther:** So which movie did you like best, *The Hobbit* or *Star Wars*?
   **Michelle:** *The Hobbit*, ³**it seems to me** / **of course**. The original *Star Wars* just looks so dated.
   **Esther:** ⁴**Not necessarily.** / **That's a good point**. *The Hobbit* movie does look more modern.

3. **Alexis:** One Direction is the best boy band ever!
   **Mother:** ⁵**Not necessarily!** / **It seems to me!** Back in my day, we loved New Kids on the Block. ⁶**That's a good point** / **As far as I'm concerned**, they're the best boy band ever!

# READING TO WRITE

**1** Number the parts of a comparison/contrast essay in order from 1–3.

_____ Give similarities and differences in two separate paragraphs.

_____ State your opinion again in a different way.

_____ State your opinion about the topic.

**2** Read the sentences that compare Hollywood movies from the United States to Bollywood movies from India. Match the sentences that are about the same topics.

**Hollywood**

1. The United States has almost 40,000 movie theaters. _f_
2. Hollywood movies make about $51 billion each year. \_\_\_\_
3. A single Hollywood film targets a specific genre, such as action, or sci-fi. \_\_\_\_
4. Hollywood makes excellent action, sci-fi, and spy movies. \_\_\_\_
5. In 2013, Hollywood produced over 600 films. \_\_\_\_
6. An average Hollywood movie costs about $47.7 million to make.

**Bollywood**

a. A single Bollywood film includes a lot of variety: musical numbers, action, comedy, and romance.
b. Bollywood produces about 1,000 films each year.
c. Bollywood movies make over $3 billion each year.
d. A Bollywood movie costs about $1.5 million to make.
e. Bollywood makes wonderful musicals with great song lyrics.
f. There are fewer than 13,000 movie theaters in India.

**3** Combine the matching sentences from Activity 2 using the *as . . . as* phrases.

| | |
|---|---|
| almost twice as many . . . as | nearly as much . . . as |
| ~~as much . . . as~~ | not as many . . . as |
| just as . . . as | nowhere near as . . . as |

1. Hollywood movies don't have _as much_ variety _as_ Bollywood movies.
2. Bollywood movies are _____ expensive to make _____ Hollywood movies.
3. There are _____ movie theaters in India _____ in the United States.
4. Bollywood films are _____ good _____ Hollywood films.
5. Bollywood films don't make _____ money _____ Hollywood movies.
6. Bollywood produces _____ films _____ Hollywood per year.

# Real or FAKE?

**Unit 1 Video 1.1**

## BEFORE YOU WATCH

1 Answer these questions about how you use the Internet.

   1. What websites do you use to get information? Name two. _____
   2. Can you tell if a digital photo has been edited? How? _____

## WHILE YOU WATCH

2 Watch the video. Are the sentences true (*T*) or false (*F*)? Correct the false sentences.

   1. Until recently, people got most of their information from books. _____
   2. In the past, it was easy to share visual information with a lot of people. _____
   3. Today, anyone can claim to be an expert. _____
   4. It's very easy now to manipulate visual information. _____
   5. Only experts can decide if something is real or fake. _____

3 Watch the video again. Complete the sentences with the words you hear.

   1. It used to take a lot of time and _____ to share information with a lot of people.
   2. Books were usually _____ by _____.
   3. But can you believe everything you _____ or _____?
   4. They are controlling the _____ so you will _____ their product.
   5. You just have to _____ attention and not _____ everything you see or read.

## AFTER YOU WATCH

4 Work with a partner. Think about where you get your information. Do you trust what you read? Why or why not?

> I go on Wikipedia sometimes to research historical events. But I know that anyone can post on Wikipedia, so I always check another source.

# Milan's FASHION WEEK

**Unit 1 Video 1.3**

## BEFORE YOU WATCH

1 **Look at the pictures and the sentences from the video. Complete the sentences with the correct words, then match the sentences to the pictures.**

a.   b.   c.

make-up    patterns    photographers

1. Lots of _____ come to Milan for Fashion Week.   ____

2. The designer Missoni is famous for his bold _____.   ____

3. It takes hours to do each model's hair and _____!   ____

## WHILE YOU WATCH

2 **Watch the video. Are the sentences true (T) or false (F)? Correct the false sentences.**

1. The blogger got a chance to go to Milan recently. _____

2. Missoni often uses bright colors in his designs. _____

3. The blogger thinks it would be cool to be a model. _____

4. A lot of the models had long hair. _____

5. There was a big dinner after the show. _____

3 **Watch the video again. Answer the questions.**

1. What does the blogger call Milan? _____

2. Who is one of the blogger's favorite designers? _____

3. Why is there a lot of waiting around before the show? _____

4. What does the blogger not have patience for? _____

5. What do the models do at the end of the show? _____

## AFTER YOU WATCH

4 **Work in small groups. Discuss how fashions have changed in the past five years. What were styles you used to think were cool, but now you'd never wear?**

> A few years ago, I used to wear really baggy jeans and big hats. I thought hoodies in really bright colors were cool – but not anymore!

# Born to DIVE

**Unit 2 Video 2.1**

## BEFORE YOU WATCH

1 **Look at these pictures from the video of a free diver. Do you think the statements are true (T) or false (F)?**

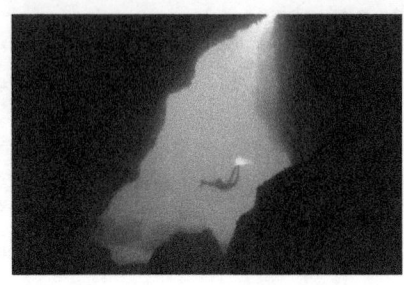

1. Free divers dive underwater on one breath of air. _____
2. Some professional free divers use equipment to help them breathe underwater. _____
3. Some free divers can stay underwater for three minutes or longer. _____

## WHILE YOU WATCH

2 **Watch the video. Circle the correct answers.**

1. Which adjective best describes Michele?
   a. shy                  b. determined            c. impatient
2. To become a professional diver, Michele must dive to a depth of more than _____ meters.
   a. 45                   b. 50                    c. 55
3. Michele's parents are _____ him.
   a. worried about        b. angry with            c. afraid of
4. Michele says his mother _____ what he does.
   a. is happy about       b. doesn't understand    c. doesn't like
5. Michele reaches _____ meters in the competition.
   a. 57                   b. 67                    c. 47

3 **Watch the video again. Check (✓) the sentences you hear.**

1. ❑ Fear is something you don't need.
2. ❑ I'm not scared because I know my limits.
3. ❑ On the day of the championship, there are big crowds.
4. ❑ He dives deep very fast.
5. ❑ His dream has finally come true!

## AFTER YOU WATCH

4 **Work with a partner. Discuss: Do you know anyone who has hurt themselves doing a sport? What happened?**

> Well, my brother broke his leg skiing a few years ago. He was going down a hill, and he hit a tree.

# Shanghai HEIGHTS

**Unit 2 Video 2.3**

## BEFORE YOU WATCH

1 Look at this picture from the video. Answer the questions.

1. Where is this man and what is he doing? _____
2. Would you like to have his job? Why or why not? _____

## WHILE YOU WATCH

2 Watch the video. Match the phrases to make true sentences.

1. Many people come to Shanghai _____
2. Sun Feng cleans the windows _____
3. He has not seen his family _____
4. He travels to his village _____
5. He is very happy _____

a. for months.
b. to hold his daughter.
c. by train.
d. to find jobs.
e. of tall buildings.

3 Watch the video again. Answer the questions.

1. Why did Sun Feng move to Shanghai? _____
2. What does he say is the worst thing about the job? _____
3. How did he feel the first time he did the job? _____
4. What does he bring home for everyone? _____
5. What does he give his father at dinner? _____

## AFTER YOU WATCH

4 Work in small groups. Discuss: Would you ever take a job far from home? What kind of job would that be?

> Yes, I would. I would take a job that was really interesting and paid a lot of money. I'd also like to live in another country.

Unit 2 | 75

# What A WASTE!

**Unit 3 Video 3.1**

## BEFORE YOU WATCH

**1 Look at these pictures from the video. Answer the questions.**

1. What do you think is going to happen to these old computers? _____

2. The picture on the right is of a *landfill* – a large trash site. What do you think the people are doing there? _____

## WHILE YOU WATCH

**2 Watch the video. Answer the questions.**

1. What is the first example of things we throw away each year? _____

2. How many cell phones do Americans throw away each day? _____

3. How many kilos of oil does it take to make one computer screen? _____

4. What could we do with our old computers? _____

5. What kind of phone is much cheaper than a new one? _____

**3 Watch the video again. Circle the words you hear.**

BILL NYE: What is e-waste?

MAN 1: Um, waste . . . **electricity / electric** that's wasted?

WOMAN 1: E-waste? **Ecology / Ecological** waste or something?

BILL NYE: Do you know what e-waste is?

WOMAN 2: Oh, maybe it's the **economic / economical** waste. Maybe like from the economy?

MAN 2: **Environment / Environmental** waste?

## AFTER YOU WATCH

**4 Work with a partner. Make a list of all your electronic devices. What will you do with them when they get old? Think of ways you could reduce your personal e-waste.**

| Device | To do |
| --- | --- |
| cell phone | donate to a charity |
| printer | return to manufacturer to recycle |

# Mission: POSSIBLE?

**Unit 3 Video 3.3**

## BEFORE YOU WATCH

**1 Read the sentences. Write the letter of the correct definition of the underlined words.**

1. Will <u>astronauts</u> ever travel to Mars? ____
2. Some people feel <u>motion sickness</u> when they try to read in a car. ____
3. Many emergency vehicles have <u>flashing</u> lights to warn people of danger. ____

a. something that appears quickly or suddenly
b. a person who travels in a spacecraft to outer space
c. a type of nausea

## WHILE YOU WATCH

**2 Watch the video. Are the sentences true (*T*) or false (*F*)? Correct the false sentences.**

1. Scientists have mastered time travel. _____
2. Traveling in space makes some astronauts sick. _____
3. The professor invented special books for astronauts to read. _____
4. One woman wore normal, clear glasses. _____
5. The woman with the flashing glasses felt good. _____

**3 Watch the video again. Answer the questions.**

1. What do many astronauts suffer from? _____
2. What was unusual about the eyes of the one astronaut? _____
3. What was the difference between the glasses the two women wore?
   _____
4. What were the women doing in the car? _____
5. Which woman became sick? _____

## AFTER YOU WATCH

**4 Work in small groups. Discuss: Do you think humans will travel to other planets in your lifetime? Where will they go first? Would you want to travel in space?**

> I think humans will go to Mars in my lifetime. Yes, I would want to travel in space, but it could be scary.

# The ORIGIN OF ARGAN OIL

Unit 4 Video 4.1

## BEFORE YOU WATCH

1 Look at the picture from the video. Answer the questions.

1. Where are these goats and what are they doing? _____

2. What are some foods we get from goats? _____

## WHILE YOU WATCH

2 Watch the video. Answer the questions.

1. What is strange about the argan trees? _____

2. What are the goats doing? _____

3. What colors are the goats? _____

4. What do people make argan oil from? _____

5. What do people use argan oil for? _____

3 Watch the video again. Put the steps of making argan oil in order.

1. First, _____        a. women roast the argan seeds over a fire.
2. Then, _____        b. they make a paste from the seeds.
3. Then, _____        c. goats eat argan fruit from a tree.
4. Next, _____        d. the women make a delicate oil.
5. Finally, _____     e. the argan fruit passes through the goats' bodies.

## AFTER YOU WATCH

4 Work with a partner. Make a list of at least three animals and what humans get from them.

| Animal | Product |
| --- | --- |
| goat | milk |
|  | cheese |
|  | meat |
|  | leather |

78 | Unit 4

# Fruits of the SEA

**Unit 4 Video 4.3**

## BEFORE YOU WATCH

**1 Look at these pictures from the video. Complete the sentences with the correct words.**

| good | islands | protein | seafood |

Japan is a group of [1]_____ surrounded by the sea. People here eat a lot of [2]_____. Fish is very [3]_____ for you. It's full of [4]_____ and vitamins. Fishing is essential to life in these islands.

## WHILE YOU WATCH

**2 Watch the video. Circle the correct words.**

1. In the first half of the video, most of the people are **young / old**.
2. Japanese people eat **10 percent / 10 tons** of all the fish caught in the world.
3. Fishermen catch squid **at night / in the morning**.
4. One of the most popular fish in Japan is the **abalone / bluefin tuna**.
5. Every day, over **40,000 / 400,000** buyers come to the Tokyo fish market.

**3 Watch the video again. Check (✓) the sentences you hear.**

1. ❑ Rich water. Water that is full of fish.
2. ❑ Life expectancy here is over 80 years old.
3. ❑ Further in, you can find squid.
4. ❑ Bluefin tuna swim in the deep waters of northern Japan.
5. ❑ There's no question of Japan's love for the sea.

## AFTER YOU WATCH

**4 Work in small groups. Discuss: Do you eat a lot of seafood? What are your favorite types? If you don't eat seafood, what are other sources of protein in your diet?**

> I eat seafood about once a week. My favorite is shrimp. I also like fried fish.

# A COOL EXPERIMENT

Unit 5 Video 5.1

## BEFORE YOU WATCH

1 Look at this graphic of global warming from the video. Do you think the sentences are true (*T*) or false (*F*)?

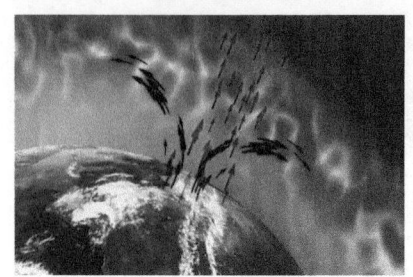

   1. Many scientists say temperatures around the world are rising. ____
   2. Greenhouse gases such as $CO_2$ and methane cool the Earth's environment. ____
   3. Humans produce greenhouse gases. ____

## WHILE YOU WATCH

2 Watch the video. Complete the sentences.

   1. Eric is going to build _____ greenhouses, each with an _____ statue.
   2. He's going to fill _____ of the greenhouses with _____ air.
   3. Each box will receive the same _____ of _____.
   4. Computers will monitor the amount of _____ in the _____.
   5. Eric _____ to be part of the _____.

3 Watch the video again. Circle any wrong words. Write the correct words on the lines.

   **Ex.:** First, he looked at the (scientist) behind it. _____*science*_____

   1. Each box must be the same. _____
   2. He'll fill one box with $CO_2$, two with methane, and one with normal air. _____
   3. They'll need special machines to make the ice boxes. _____
   4. After four-and-a-half hours, the ice statues start to melt! _____
   5. Methane and $CO_2$ are major culprits for global warming. _____

## AFTER YOU WATCH

4 Work in small groups. Discuss: Do temperatures seem to be rising where you live? Are there more storms and floods where you live than there were several years ago?

   > I'm not sure. I think temperatures are a little warmer. We did have two big storms last year. My aunt's house was flooded.

# Trendsetters

**Unit 5 Video 5.3**

## BEFORE YOU WATCH

1 Look at these pictures from the video and read the definition. Then answer the question.

> **Trendsetter** /'trend' setər/ (noun)
> a person, organization, etc., that starts to do something that others then copy

These girls are *trendsetters* in Japan. Think of a recent trend in your school. How and where did it start?

_____

## WHILE YOU WATCH

2 Watch the video. Circle the correct adverbs.

1. In Japan, trends are **nearly / really** vital.
2. The opinions of trendsetters are **slightly / extremely** important to companies.
3. The girls are **absolutely / somewhat** impressed by the video booth.
4. They think that the photo booth is **pretty / slightly** easier to use.
5. The girls are **very / hardly** excited to meet their friends.

3 Watch the video again. Answer the questions.

1. Where do the two girls live? _____
2. What do companies in Japan want to know? _____
3. What are the girls testing today? _____
4. Which booth do the girls prefer? _____
5. Why do companies care what Saeko and Yuko think about new products?
   _____

## AFTER YOU WATCH

4 Work with a partner. Make an advertisement for a new trend, such as a new style of shoes or a new smart device. Include graphics and text. Share your advertisement with the class.

This page intentionally left blank.

# Irregular verbs

| Base Verb | Simple Past | Past Participle |
|---|---|---|
| babysit | babysat | babysat |
| be | was, were | been |
| beat | beat | beat |
| become | became | become |
| begin | began | begun |
| bite | bit | bitten |
| bleed | bled | bled |
| blow | blew | blown |
| break | broke | broken |
| bring | brought | brought |
| build | built | built |
| burn | burned | burned/burnt |
| buy | bought | bought |
| catch | caught | caught |
| choose | chose | chosen |
| come | came | come |
| cost | cost | cost |
| cut | cut | cut |
| deal | dealt | dealt |
| dive | dived/dove | dived |
| do | did | done |
| draw | drew | drawn |
| dream | dreamed/dreamt | dreamed/dreamt |
| drink | drank | drunk |
| drive | drove | driven |
| eat | ate | eaten |
| fall | fell | fallen |
| feel | felt | felt |
| fight | fought | fought |
| find | found | found |
| fit | fit | fit |
| fly | flew | flown |
| forget | forgot | forgotten |
| freeze | froze | frozen |
| get | got | gotten |
| give | gave | given |
| go | went | gone |
| grow | grew | grown |
| hang | hung | hung |
| have | had | had |
| hear | heard | heard |
| hide | hid | hidden |
| hit | hit | hit |
| hold | held | held |
| hurt | hurt | hurt |
| keep | kept | kept |
| know | knew | known |
| lead | led | led |

| Base Verb | Simple Past | Past Participle |
|---|---|---|
| leave | left | left |
| let | let | let |
| lie | lay | lain |
| light | lit | lit |
| lose | lost | lost |
| make | made | made |
| mean | meant | meant |
| meet | met | met |
| pay | paid | paid |
| prove | proved | proven |
| put | put | put |
| quit | quit | quit |
| read | read | read |
| ride | rode | ridden |
| ring | rang | rung |
| rise | rose | risen |
| run | ran | run |
| say | said | said |
| see | saw | seen |
| sell | sold | sold |
| send | sent | sent |
| set | set | set |
| shoot | shot | shot |
| show | showed | shown |
| shut | shut | shut |
| sing | sang | sung |
| sink | sank | sunk |
| sit | sat | sat |
| sleep | slept | slept |
| speak | spoke | spoken |
| spend | spent | spent |
| spread | spread | spread |
| stand | stood | stood |
| steal | stole | stolen |
| stick | stuck | stuck |
| strike | struck | struck/stricken |
| swim | swam | swum |
| take | took | taken |
| teach | taught | taught |
| tell | told | told |
| think | thought | thought |
| throw | threw | thrown |
| understand | understood | understood |
| wake | woke | woken |
| wear | wore | worn |
| win | won | won |
| write | wrote | written |

# Credits

The authors and publishers acknowledge the following sources of copyright material and are grateful for the permissions granted. While every effort has been made, it has not always been possible to identify the sources of all the material used, or to trace all copyright holders. If any omissions are brought to our notice, we will be happy to include the appropriate acknowledgements on reprinting.

p. 2-3 (B/G): Getty Images/Ian McKinnell; p. 3 (1): Shutterstock Images/RossHelen; p. 3 (2): Shutterstock Images/enciktat; p. 3 (3): Alamy/©Tatiana Morozova; p. 3 (4): Shutterstock Images/Fotogenix; p. 3 (5): Corbis/W2 Photography; p. 4 (L): Getty Images/murat sarica; p. 4 (B/G): Shutterstock Images/Pixsooz; p. 5 (R): Shutterstock Images/marekuliasz; p. 6 (TL): Alamy/©ClassicStock; p. 6 (TCL): Shutterstock Images/Hector Sanchez; p. 6 (BCL): Shutterstock Images/Filip Fuxa; p. 6 (TBL): Alamy/©trekkerimages; p. 6 (BL): Getty Images/TimZillion; p. 7 (R): Shutterstock Images/CroMary; p. 8 (BL): Getty Images/Julia Fishkin; p. 8 (BR): Getty Images/Denis O'Regan; p. 9 (TL): Getty Images/T.J. Kirkpatrick; p. 10 (TL): Getty Images/Charles Gullung; p. 10 (CL): Alamy/©Frances Roberts; p. 10 (C): Alamy/©moodboard; p. 10 (B/G): Shutterstock Images/nikkytok; p. 12 (B/G): Alamy/©Stock Foundry Images; p. 13 (a): Getty Images/Aminart; p. 13 (b): Alamy/©Hero Images Inc.; p. 13 (c): Getty Images/DragonImages; p. 13 (d): Alamy/©STOCK4B GmbH; p. 13 (e): Alamy/©Bob Ebbesen; p. 14 (L): Darío Rodríguez/DESNIVEL./Courtesy of Robyn Raboutou; p. 15 (R): Getty Images/zhekos; p. 16 (TL): Getty Images/Tetra Images; p. 17 (L): Shutterstock Images/traithep khamiptoon; p. 18 (TL): Alamy/©PhotoAlto; p. 18 (BL): Shutterstock Images/Oleg Vinnichenko; p. 19 (TR): Getty Images/sturti; p. 20 (CR): Getty Images/Dimitri Otis; p. 20 (TR, B/G): Alamy/©Sabena Jane Blackbird; p. 20 (TL): Alamy/©Greenshoots Communications; p. 22 (B/G): Alamy/©Michael Doolittle; p. 23 (a): Shutterstock Images/koosen; p. 23 (b): Alamy/©David Askham; p. 23 (c): Alamy/©imageBROKER; p. 23 (d): Alamy/©Jochen Tack; p. 23 (e): Shutterstock Images/Ken Reid; p. 23 (BR): Shutterstock Images/PT Images; p. 24 (TL): Shutterstock Images/Ahturner; p. 24 (CL): NASA; p. 24 (BL): NASA; p. 24 (B/G): Shutterstock Images/JaySi; p. 25 (R): Alamy/©Kevin Galvin; p. 26 (TL): Alamy/©GARY DOAK; p. 26 (a): Shutterstock Images/Elnur; p. 26 (b): Getty Images/Kali Nine LLC; p. 26 (c): Alamy/©Kip Evans; p. 26 (d): Shutterstock Images/Amble Design; p. 26 (e): Shutterstock Images/Volt Collection; p. 26 (f): Getty Images/Anatoliy Babiy; p. 26 (g): Alamy/©ZUMA Press, Inc.; p. 26 (h): Shutterstock Images/Stephen Coburn; p. 28 (TL): Getty Images/Jamie Grill; p. 28 (CL): Shutterstock Images/Nadiia Korol; p. 28 (BL): Shutterstock Images/cocoo; p. 29 (TL): Shutterstock Images/Goodluz; p. 30 (TL): Getty Images/Niklas Halle'n/Barcroft India/Barcroft Media; p. 30 (CR): Sascha Baumann/Getty Images; p. 30 (TR, B/G): Shutterstock Images/Evgeny Karandaev; p. 32 (B/G): Getty Images/Hemant Mehta; p. 33 (1): Shutterstock Images/Andrey Armyagov; p. 33 (2): Getty Images/Peter Johansky; p. 33 (3): Shutterstock Images/Joe Belanger; p. 33 (4): Shutterstock Images/L. Kragt Bakker; p. 33 (5): Shutterstock Images/Sheila_Fitzgerald; p. 33 (6): Shutterstock Images/Masson; p. 33 (7): Alamy/©Profimedia.CZ a.s.; p. 33 (8): Alamy/©Studio51; p. 33 (9): Shutterstock Images/Catalin Petolea; p. 34 (TL): Shutterstock Images/Nomad_Soul; p. 34 (TR): YOSHIKAZU TSUNO/AFP/GettyImages; p. 34 (BL): Shutterstock Images/SAAC; p. 34 (BR): Shutterstock Images/M. Unal Ozmen; p. 36 (TL): Getty Images/Andy Reynolds; p. 36 (a): Getty Images/C_yung; p. 36 (b): Shutterstock Images/Isantilli; p. 36 (c): Getty Images/Dennis Gottlieb; p. 36 (d): Getty Images/Kate Baldwin; p. 36 (e): Shutterstock Images/Chad Zuber; p. 36 (f): Getty Images/Nicole S. Young; p. 37 (R): Shutterstock Images/Alexeysun; p. 38 (TL): Shutterstock Images/Robnroll; p. 38 (BL): Alamy/©Bon Appetit; p. 39 (TR): Shutterstock Images/Joe Gough; p. 40 (B/G): Shutterstock Images/wavebreakmedia; p. 40 (TL): Shutterstock Images/kai keisuke; p. 40 (CL): Getty Images/pictafolio; p. 40 (TC): Getty Images/Arnold H. Drapkin; p. 40 (TR): Alamy/©Mahdees Mahjoob; p. 40 (CR): Alamy/©Mode Images; p. 42 (B/G): Getty Images/Peter Dazeley; p. 44 (TL): Getty Images/L.Cohen/WireImage/Nordstrom; p. 44 (CL): Getty Images/STEPHANE DE SAKUTIN/AFP; p. 44 (BL): Getty Images/Harry How; p. 45 (R): Alamy/©lemonade; p. 46 (TL): Getty Images/urfinguss; p. 46 (BL): Shutterstock Images/cromic; p. 48 (TL): Alamy/©ALAN EDWARDS; p. 48 (CL): Getty Images/Logan Fazio/FilmMagic; p. 48 (BL): Getty Images/Peter Kramer/NBC/NBC NewsWire; p. 49 (C): Markus Mainka/Shutterstock; p. 49 (B): Steve Collender/Shutterstock; p. 49 (TR): Shutterstock Images/joycedragan; p. 50 (TR): Getty Images/Peter Dazeley; p. 50 (C): Getty Images/Brad Barket; p. 50 (BR): Shutterstock Images/Helga Esteb; p. 50 (B/G): Shutterstock Images/Apples Eyes Studio; p. 52 (B/G): Getty Images/Kevin Elvis King; p. 54 (B/G): Alamy/©Peter M. Wilson; p. 55 (1): Shutterstock Images/Michael Dechev; p. 55 (2): Shutterstock Images/Sanit Fuangnakhon; p. 55 (3): Shutterstock Images/Filip Bjorkman; p. 55 (4): Shutterstock Images/Cynoclub; p. 55 (5): Shutterstock Images/Chimpinski; p. 55 (6): Shutterstock Images/Olga Popova; p. 55 (7): Shutterstock Images/Minerva Studio; p. 55 (8): Shutterstock Images/Darren Pullman; p. 55 (9): Getty Images/Pulse/Fuse; p. 55 (10): Shutterstock Images/Ivaschenko Roman; p. 56 (L): Corbis/©ROLEX DELA PENA/epa; p. 56 (R): Corbis/©DIVYAKANT SOLANKI/epa; p. 58 (TL): Alamy/©Idealink Photography; p. 59 (R): Getty Images/toddmedia; p. 60 (TL): Alamy/©B.O'Kane; p. 61 (TR): Shutterstock Images/fotoslaz; p. 61 (TL): Shutterstock Images/Olga Knutova; p. 62 (L): Alamy/©The Art Archive; p. 62 (CL): Alamy/©Francesco Gustincich; p. 62 (CR): Corbis/©NingJie; p. 62 (R): Shutterstock Images/Igor Kovalchuk; p. 62 (B/G): Shutterstock Images/Fedor Selivanov; p. 64 (B/G) Corbis/ROBIN UTRECHT FOTOGRAFIE/HillCreek Pictures; p. 65 (1): Getty Images/Jupiterimages; p. 65 (2): Getty Images/ERproductions Ltd; p. 65 (3): Alamy/©Tony Watson; p. 65 (4): Shutterstock Images/Taras Vyshnya; p. 65 (5): Getty Images/Image Source; p. 65 (6): Alamy/©Blue Jean Images; p. 65 (7): Shutterstock Images/Richard Thornton; p. 65 (8): Alamy/©Datacraft - QxQ images; p. 65 (9): Corbis/Roger Brooks; p. 66 (T): Shutterstock Images/gualtiero boffi; p. 66 (TR): Corbis/Jon-Michael Sullivan/Staff; p. 66 (L): Shutterstock Images/HomeStudio; p. 66 (BR): Shutterstock Images/Mike Degteariov; p. 67 (R): Getty Images/mediaphotos; p. 67 (CR): Shutterstock Images/Dan Kosmayer; p. 68 (TL): Shutterstock Images/topten22photo; p. 68 (TCL): Alamy/©FocusChina; p. 68 (BCL): Shutterstock Images/Paolo Bona; p. 68 (BL): Alamy/©ZUMA Press, Inc.; p. 69 (R): Alamy/©Rob Crandall; p. 70 (L): Alamy/©ImagesBazaar; p. 71 (TR): Alamy/©Corbis Super RF; p. 72 (TR): Getty Images/Chung Sung-Jun; p. 72 (TC): Getty Images/Chung Sung-Jun; p. 72 (C): Shutterstock Images/Soultkd; p. 72 (B/G): Shutterstock Images/leungchopan; p. 74 (B/G): Getty Images/Borut Furlan; p. 76 (L): Getty Images/New York Daily News Archive/contributor; p. 76 (CL): Alamy/©Randy Duchaine; p. 76 (R): Getty Images/Maremagnum; p. 77 (L): Shutterstock Images/MichaelTaylor; p. 78 (T): Getty Images/Joseph Devenney; p. 78 (BL): Getty Images/Carol Yepes; p. 80 (CL): Alamy/©Ingram Publishing; p. 80 (BL): Alamy/©Nature Picture Library; p. 81 (TL): Shutterstock Images/cenap refik ongan; p. 81 (BL): Shutterstock Images/NorGal; p. 81 (TR): Getty Images/Thinkstock/Sini?a Bota?; p. 82 (TR, B/G): Image courtesy of the Beinecke Library; p. 82 (L): Image courtesy of the Beinecke Library; p. 84 (B/G): Getty Images/John Lund; p. 85 (L): Alamy/©Everett Collection Inc; p. 85 (BL): Studio Works; p. 85 (BC): Alamy/©Ben Molyneux; p. 85 (BR): Corbis/©Bettmann; p. 86 (T): Shutterstock Images/MaxyM; p. 86 (L): Shutterstock Images/Emilio100; p. 87 (R): Shutterstock Images/M. Unal Ozmen; p. 88 (L): Shutterstock Images/Soumitra Pendse; p. 89 (1): Getty Images/Cavan Images; p. 89 (2): Shutterstock Images/Kingarion; p. 89 (3): Alamy/©Trinity Mirror/Mirrorpix; p. 90 (TL): Corbis/©Bettmann; p. 91 (TR): Shutterstock Images/Stacy Barnett; p. 92 (T): Shutterstock Images/MaraZe; p. 92 (TL): Shutterstock Images/kravka; p. 92 (CL): Getty Images/Witold Skrypczak; p. 92 (C): Alamy/©Emily Riddell; p. 92 (CR): Getty Images/traveler1116; p. 92 (B/G): Shutterstock Images/Aivoges; p. 92 (BL): Shutterstock Images/Kravka; p. 94 (B/G): Corbis/©Juice Images; p. 95 (T): Shutterstock Images/Air Images; p. 95 (TR): Shutterstock Images/wavebreakmedia; p. 95 (CR): Alamy/©Jeff Morgan 16; p. 95 (BR): Getty Images/moodboard; p. 96 (TL): Alamy/©Juice Images; p. 96 (CL): Shutterstock Images/Peter Gudella; p. 96 (BL): Shutterstock Images/donatas1205; p. 97 (B): Alamy/©B Christopher; p. 98 (T): Shutterstock Images/Africa Studio; p. 98 (1): Shutterstock Images/Africa Studio; p. 98 (2): Shutterstock Images/racorn; p. 98 (3): Getty Images/VikZa; p. 98 (4): Getty Images/Jetta Productions; p. 98 (5): Shutterstock Images/Izf; p. 98 (6): Getty Images/Digital Vision.; p. 98 (7): Alamy/©David Young-Wolff; p. 98 (8): Shutterstock Images/Sasha Samardzija; p. 98 (9): Alamy/©Ira Berger; p. 98 (BL): Alamy/©GraficallyMinded; p. 99 (L): Getty Images/Cultura/Leon Harris; p. 100 (TL): Shutterstock Images/Jultud; p. 100 (TCL): Shutterstock Images/Fetullah Mercan; p. 100 (CL): Getty Images/Nightscorp; p. 100 (BCL): Shutterstock Images/Charles Mann; p. 100 (TL): Shutterstock Images/Everything; p. 101 (TL): Alamy/©dpa picture alliance archive; p. 102 (TL): Getty Images/Pamela Martin; p. 102 (CL): Getty Images/Brendon Thorne; p. 102 (BL): Getty Images/Al Bello; p. 102 (B/G): Shutterstock Images/Marish; p. 104 (B/G): Corbis/©Arctic-Images; p. 119 (TR): Shutterstock Images/Lucy; p. 119 (CR): Shutterstock Images/American Spirit; p. 120 (BR): Shutterstock Images/wandee007; Back cover: Shutterstock Images/Cbenjasuwan.

Front cover photography by Alamy/©Image Source Plus.

**The publishers are grateful to the following illustrators:**
Anni Betts: p. 50, 86, 99; Q2A Media Services, Inc.: p. 27, 43, 58, 73, 75, 116, 117, 118, 120.

**All video stills by kind permission of:**
Discovery Communications, LLC 2015: p. 2 (1, 3), 5, 10, 12 (1, 3, 4), 15, 20, 21, 22 (1, 3), 25, 30, 32 (1, 3, 4), 35, 40, 41, 42 (1, 3), 45, 50, 54 (1, 3, 4), 57, 62, 63, 64 (1, 3), 67, 72, 74 (1, 3, 4), 77, 82, 83, 84 (1, 3), 87, 92, 94 (1, 3, 4), 97, 102, 103, 116, 117, 118, 119, 120; Cambridge University Press: p. 2 (2), 8, 12 (2), 18, 22 (2), 28, 32 (2), 38, 42 (2), 48, 54 (2), 60, 63 (2), 70, 74 (2), 80, 84 (2), 90, 94 (2), 100.

# Credits

The authors and publishers acknowledge the following sources of copyright material and are grateful for the permissions granted. While every effort has been made, it has not always been possible to identify the sources of all the material used, or to trace all copyright holders. If any omissions are brought to our notice, we will be happy to include the appropriate acknowledgements on reprinting.

p. 5 (BL): Alamy/©Jan Wlodarczyk; p. 7 (CL): Getty Images/Henrik Sorensen; p. 9 (BL): Getty Images/Zoranm; p. 15 (TL): Shutterstock/Testing; p. 16 (TL): Shutterstock/CandyBox Images; p. 17 (CL): Getty Images/M-imagephotography/iStockphoto; p. 18 (A): Getty Images/Hero Images; p. 18 (B): Shuttertstock/Jianghaistudio; p. 18 (C): Shutterstock/Halfpoint; p. 18 (D): Getty Images/Joel Eichler; p. 18 (E): Getty Images/Mark Bowden; p. 18 (F): Alamy/©Hero Images Inc.; p. 18 (G): Shutterstock/William Perugini; p. 18 (H): Shutterstock/Bikeriderlondon; p. 21 (CR): Shutterstock/Sean Locke Photography; p. 22 (1): Shutterstock/Yuriy Rudyy; p. 22 (2): Shutterstock/Photographee.eu; p. 22 (3): Shutterstock/Sergey Ryzhov; p. 22 (4): Shutterstock/Iakov Filimonov; p. 22 (5): Shutterstock/Photographee.eu; p. 22 (6): Shutterstock/ffolas; p. 22 (7): Shutterstock/Africa Studio; p. 22 (8): Getty Images/Ryerson Clark; p. 22 (9): Getty Images/Dennis Hoyne; p. 23 (TR): Shutterstock/Jacek Chabraszewski; p. 27 (CR): Shutterstock/Ulga; p. 30 (CL): Getty Images/PhotoAlto/Frederic Cirou; p. 31 (CL): Shutterstock/Konrad Mostert; p. 35 (C): Getty Images/DreamPictures; p. 36 (1): Shutterstock/Nickolay Khoroshkov; p. 36 (2): Shutterstock/R. MACKAY PHOTOGRAPHY, LLC; p. 36 (3): Shutterstock/Nikita Rogul; p. 36 (4): Getty Images/phanlop888/iStockphoto; p. 36 (5): Shutterstock/Maggee; p. 36 (6): Shutterstock/Africa Studio; p. 36 (7): Shutterstock/Mdblk1984; p. 36 (8): Shutterstock/Olga Kovalenko; p. 36 (9): Shutterstock/Olga Popova; p. 36 (10): Alamy/©Corbis Super; p. 41 (TR): Shutterstock/Igor Lateci; Shutterstock/sunlight77; p. 46 (CL): Shutterstock/PAUL ATKINSON; p. 47 (CR): Alamy/©Renato Granieri; p. 50 (TR): Alamy/©David Parker; p. 62 (CT): Getty Images/Andy Shaw/Bloomberg; p. 63 (CL): Alamy/©Paolo Patrizi; p. 69 (CR): Alamy/©ZUMA Press, Inc.; p. 70 (1): Alamy/©Gabe Palmer; p. 70 (2): Shutterstock/Valeriy Velikov; p. 70 (3): Getty Images/Steve Debenport; p. 70 (4): Shutterstock/Stasique; p. 70 (5): Alamy/©fStop Images GmbH; p. 70 (6): Shutterstock/Rido; p. 70 (7): Shutterstock/scyther5; p. 70 (8): Shutterstock/Andrey_Popov.

Front cover photography by Alamy/©Image Source Plus.

**The publishers are grateful to the following illustrators:**

Q2A Media Services, Inc.

**All video stills by kind permission of Discovery Communications, LLC 2015.**

# Notes

# Notes

# Notes

# Notes

# Notes